PENGUIN BOOKS

THE TASTE OF WORDS

Raza Mir teaches management at William Paterson University, USA. He is the co-author of *Anthems of Resistance: A Celebration of Progressive Urdu Poetry*. He can be reached at urduwallah@gmail.com.

THE TASTE
OF WORDS

AN INTRODUCTION TO URDU POETRY

Edited and Translated by

RAZA MIR

Foreword by GULZAR

PENGUIN BOOKS

An imprint of Penguin Random House

PENGUIN BOOKS

USA | Canada | UK | Ireland | Australia
New Zealand | India | South Africa | China | Singapore

Penguin Books is part of the Penguin Random House group of companies
whose addresses can be found at global.penguinrandomhouse.com

Published by Penguin Random House India Pvt. Ltd
4th Floor, Capital Tower 1, MG Road,
Gurugram 122 002, Haryana, India

First published by Penguin Books India 2014

Anthology copyright © Penguin Books India 2014
Introduction and Translation copyright © Raza Mir 2014
Foreword copyright © Gulzar 2014
The copyright for the individual poems vests with the respective poets or their
heirs/estates
Page 293 is an extension of the copyright page

10 9 8 7 6 5 4 3 2

ISBN 9780143421184

Typeset in Sabon by Eleven Arts, Delhi

Printed at Manipal Technologies Limited, India

www.penguin.co.in

CONTENTS

FOREWORD

Urdu is a nation unto itself. Wherever it travels, it creates its own world. It was born in India, but does not belong to India alone. It is the official language of Pakistan, but does not belong to Pakistan alone. When it reached Oslo (Norway), it settled there. It went to Great Britain, and created its own home. It reached Canada, and a community emerged. It reached the United States, and became a native tongue. For it was embraced by Raza Mir.

The truth is that instead of 'embraced', if we could use a different metaphor, we would say 'adopted by lips'. Wherever Urdu goes, it clasps people in a bear hug. It becomes a tradition unto itself. For Urdu is after all, the lingua franca of a culture.

URDU

> *Ye kaisa ishq hai Urdu zaban ka*
> *Maza ghulta ha lafzon ka zaban par*
> *Ke jaise paan mein mehnga khimaam ghulta hai*
> *Nasha aata hai Urdu bolne mein*
> *Gilori ki tarah hain moonh lagi sab istelaahen*
> *Lutf deti hain*
>
> *Halaq chhooti hai Urdu to*
> *Halaq se jaise mai ka ghoont utarta hai*

Badi 'aristocracy' hai zaban mein
Faqeeri mein nawaabi ka maza deti hai Urdu

Agarche maani kam hote hain aur alfaaz ki
     ifraat hoti hai
Magar phir bhi . . .
Buland aawaaz padhiye to bahut hi motabar lagti
     hain baatein
Kahin kuchh door se kaanon mein padhti hai agar Urdu
To lagta hai
Ke din jaadon ke hain, khidki khuli hai, dhoop
     andar aa rahi hai

Ajab hai ye zaban Urdu
Kabhi yoonhi safar karte
Agar koi musafir sher padh de Mir, Ghalib ka
Vo chaahe ajnabi ho
Yahi lagta hai vo mere vatan ka hai
Bade shaista lahje mein kisi se Urdu sun kar
     kya nahin lagta
Ke ek tehzeeb ki aawaaz hai Urdu!!

Janaab Raza Mir, Urdu mein aap ka hissa yaad
     rahega.

URDU

What is this love of Urdu
That the taste of words dissolves on the tongue
Like expensive tobacco dissolves with a bite of paan?
Urdu speech produces a mellow high,
Like the many flavours of a delectable morsel of betel
That frolic in the mouth.

When Urdu touches the throat
It descends like a sip of wine.
A strange aristocracy it possesses
That, even in penury, Urdu yields a sense of immense
        prestige.

Though, at times, there is a paucity of meaning
And a surfeit of words,
But even so . . .
When declaimed in a firm voice, words appear
weighty and solemn
When Urdu reaches the ears from a distance
It appears
As if on winter days, the window is open and
        sunshine is pouring in.

Strange is this Urdu tongue
That, when on a journey,
Should a wayfarer declaim a couplet from Mir, from Ghalib,
Be that a complete stranger
He still appears a compatriot.

Does it not feel
That the lingua franca of a culture is this Urdu!
Janaab Raza Mir, I will remember your role in Urdu.[1]

                                                Gulzar

PREFACE

This is first and foremost a gift for my wife Farah. It was she who laid out the idea of this book for me in detail, as a volume that would not only help her dip her toe in the vast ocean that constituted Urdu poetry, but also provide her with an entry point into the language itself, with its occasionally intimidating metaphors and linguistic peculiarities.

Like Farah, I know a lot of people whose interest in Urdu poetry vastly exceeds their ability to engage with it, partly because of their unfamiliarity with the script, but also because of its often mystifying and outsider-unfriendly albeit tantalizing metaphorical conventions. Indeed, I am one of them. In school, I formally studied Hindi and Telugu, and despite Urdu being my putative mother tongue, I never engaged with it (except orally) till I was in my teens. It is only my unhealthy obsession with Urdu poetry that finally forced me to teach myself the Urdu script, and resolve the helplessness I felt when the joy of hearing a good poem was rendered ephemeral by my illiteracy. While my ineptitude with regard to Urdu poetry has been happily resolved, it obviously persists in other theatres—such as when I attend a Carnatic music concert, and watch the cognoscenti among the listeners keep beat with their palms and speak of kritis and adi-taalam, while all I can say is 'That sounded nice!' I would also love to read a good book on relatively alien cultural traditions, albeit one that is not too dense and impenetrable, with lines like:

'One *margam* of Bharatanatyam consists of *allaripu, jatiswaram, sabdam, varnam* and *tillana*.' I hope I will not bamboozle you in this book with unexplained references to *radif, qafiya, musaddas* or such technicalities. This book seeks to enhance your affective enjoyment of Urdu poetry, with as little interference from me as possible.

The intended readership of this book does not necessarily comprise Urdu experts or those who have read a lot of Urdu poetry in the original. Rather, I visualize an intelligent reader who, while interested in poetry as a genre, may not have a working knowledge of the Urdu script, and may not even be familiar with or fluent in Devanagri either. They would have read poetry in English and other languages to varying extents, but their exposure to Urdu might primarily be oral (Indian film songs, CDs of ghazals and poetry, the company of Urdu-literate friends). They do enjoy the spoken cadence of the language, but might have been deprived of the non-trivial pleasure that comes from a reflective reading of the poems.

In this anthology, I have attempted to provide an entry point to Urdu poetry for such interested non-insiders. To these readers, I offer a quasi-formal introduction to the canon and the contemporary landscape of Urdu poetry, with a highly arbitrary and subjective selection of around 150 poems from approximately fifty poets. Many of these poems have been abridged due to space considerations. I begin with a brief historical essay on Urdu and Urdu poetry (which is quirky, idiosyncratic, contingent and incomplete, but hopefully interesting) before laying out my selection of poems. I am also happy to offer a brief Internet roadmap of websites where one can read more about the poets and find more translated work. I have also identified websites in the public domain where these poems can be heard and viewed as performance. I have included biographical notes on the poets, which are not meant to be exhaustive, but just an attempt to render them human enough. The poets are ordered chronologically; and while I have chosen the list with care, there will obviously be omissions, of poems and poets, that some readers will consider unforgivable. If reviewers of this book express anger over the fact that I overlooked certain poets, poems or verses (or was foolish enough to include some 'lightweight' in this august company), I will be delighted. For in my wilder dreams, I envisage a series of sequel anthologies, like a good B-grade Hollywood horror film franchise, which people will disparage, but will be drawn to, as if to unhealthy street food. So do drum up the outrage. I briefly considered ignoring Ghalib in my selection to ensure such a backlash, but there is a line between quirkiness and insanity that even I am aware of!

I would also like to eschew any claims of genre-originality. This task of popularizing Urdu among its script-challenged enthusiasts is not new. As I have mentioned, I myself grew up without learning the Urdu script formally, and am indebted to a host of teachers.[1]

In this collection, I have tried to accomplish three inter-related tasks. First, readers can use this volume as a rudimentary dictionary, a source of learning Urdu, or a way of engaging more organically and contextually with the words in a poem. The Internet roadmap adds greater charm to the experience: for example, it is fun to read Amir Khusrau's thirteenth-century *qawwali* (for instance, '*Chhap tilak sab cheeni re . . .*') in translation, but the charm is infinitely multiplied if one can do so while listening to it being belted out by Abida Parveen!

The second task that I have set myself is that of translating in an idiom that is accessible to a relatively heterogeneous readership. It is here that I have had to make some difficult choices. Should one translate poetry as rhyme to reflect its potential 'singability' (and risk it degenerating occasionally into doggerel)? Or should one strive to preserve the verbal integrity of the poem and eschew rhyme and metre, in the hope that readers will understand the underlying poetics by themselves? Not only did I mentally agonize over this question, I actually wrote the entire first draft of this book as free verse, before deciding impulsively that, sometimes, 'not to rhyme, was a cryme' (indulge my puns, please!). Thus I chose to retranslate several—but by no means all—poems rhythmically. Even when I have tried my hand at rhyme, I have done my best to not inject myself, the translator, into the relationship between the poet and the reader. You will be the final arbiter of whether my choice has worked out.

I also want to raise the tricky issue of the transliteration scheme to be adopted. A number of formats have been proposed by academics dealing with Urdu, many of them highly precise and consistent. However, they tend to be themselves very arcane and intimidating to the eye. To maintain the popular flavour of the book, I have deliberately chosen to go with an unscientific, 'vernacular' format. My schema (if I may call it one) is derived from the way in which Hindustani words have been portrayed in movie posters in India over the years. For instance, a standard transliteration scheme deployed by the *Annual of Urdu Studies*, a respected journal, would represent a line from a song in the film *Hum Dono* as: 'Har fikr kō dhûêN mēN urātā čalā gayā'. I would have instead gone in this book with: '*Har fikr ko dhuen mein udaata chalaa gayaa*'. Readers from the subcontinent, who are in the habit of reading transliterated movie posters and advertisements, will be familiar with this format. I beg the indulgence of others, on the plea that those who are finicky about transliteration are usually familiar with the original script, and can therefore make do with the originals.

Finally, this book is an attempt to build another tiny bridge between the modern subcontinent and a language that is currently under siege on a variety of fronts. In the recent past, Urdu has struggled to gain acceptance from elitist rulers, dismissive linguists and political conservatives who have either sought to belittle it as a crude indistinct dialect or tainted it by association with putatively traitorous minorities. What has led to its survival in the South Asian landscape is the fact that it was embraced by the masses, and has remained alive as a spoken tongue. Perhaps reflecting this public-oriented ethos, its literary tradition, especially its poetic tradition, is simultaneously erudite and accessible, with a rhythm that can be intoned by a theologian and also sung by a street beggar. From culturally mobile ambiguities in words like *sanam* (simultaneously meaning 'beloved' and 'stone') to geographically ubiquitous slogans like '*Inquilab Zindabad*' ('Long Live the Revolution'), Urdu is a part of the lived experience of the Indian subcontinent, even among those who seek to deny and denigrate it. This book is my attempt to keep the language alive among its westernized friends as well. I hope you like it.

INTRODUCTION
THE FLUTTER OF ANGEL WINGS

Naddi ka mod, chashma-e shireen ka zer-o-bam
Chaadar shab-e nujoom ki, shabnam ka rakht-e nam
Moti ki aab, gul ki mehak, maah-e nau ka kham
In sab ke imtezaaj se paida hui hai tu
Kitne haseen ufaq se huvaida hui hai tu

Lehja maleeh hai ke namak-khwaar hoon tera
Sehat zaban mein hai ke beemar hoon tera
Aazad-e sher hoon ke giraftar hoon tera
Tere karam se sher-o-sukhan ka imam hoon
Shahon pe khandazan hoon ke tera ghulam hoon

The bend of the river, and the stream's bubbly path
The veil of the starry night, and the moist dew of the morn
The pearl's clarity, rose's fragrance and the new moon's swathe
All came together harmoniously and you were born
What a beauteous horizon have you arisen from!

Sweet is my speech for having tasted of your salt[1]
Healthy my tongue that I am ill with love for you
My verse flies free, for I am entombed in your vault
It is your boon that I rule the realm of poetry too
I mock the kings now that I am your slave.

1

This beautiful ode to Urdu, written by Josh Malihabadi, was never published, but has found its way to Urdu lovers over time through a rich oral tradition.[2]

Contrast this verse with the playful comedy of Dilawar Figaar, a Pakistani poet who laments the replacement of Urdu by English in common usage. Here are two *shers* (couplets) from his poem 'Pure Ghazal in Urdu' that exemplify how English has been incorporated into daily speech alongside colloquial Urdu:

Na ho jab heart in the chest, *phir* tongue in the mouth *kyon*?
To beautify this line, throw some light in Urdu
There should be *yaqeenan* no *milawat* in the literature
Therefore I never call *shab ko*[3] night in Urdu.

Urdu has prided itself on its mongrel roots and cosmopolitan ethos. It was never a language of kings and courts (though a surprising number of rulers tried their hand at Urdu poetry), nor did it confine itself to any religion (despite its deployment by communalists and divisive rulers to drive a wedge between communities). It is a quintessentially modern language, with neither a distinct writing style (no formalized diacritics, and a borrowed script) nor any claim to a direct link with a root language. To chart the emergence of Urdu is itself a fraught task, full of political pitfalls and contradictions. The progression between Hindavi, Rekhti and Urdu is a continuous one, and to break that continuity into a linguistic taxonomy is an act of social construction that is neither helpful nor productive. In this anthology, for instance, I have included Amir Khusrau, who lived in the thirteenth century, as an Urdu poet. Others may choose the sixteenth-century Deccan king Quli Qutub Shah as an originary Urdu poet, while some may play safer and commence with the seventeenth-century poet Wali Dakkani. At any rate, it is correct to say that the language has primarily thrived through an oral tradition, much of which is predicated on its poetry. That tradition has always been engaged with the direct reality of its purveyors, and I would venture to say that the best Urdu poetry is rarely the kind that is steeped in metaphysics, but one which talks of real issues: love and other relationships, jobs and occupations, bazaar scenes, feelings of marginality and oppression, revolution, the yearning of enslaved people to be free, and matters of religion (not metaphysical exegeses but rather matters of practice, celebrations of martyrs and making fun of hypocritical proselytizers).

In this introductory essay, I make no claims to comprehensiveness or neutrality. I just offer you a contingent and partisan analysis of what I consider to be important milestones in the dynamic trajectories of Urdu poetry.

The period between the thirteenth and the sixteenth centuries CE can be said to mark Urdu's prehistory, where the language existed primarily as consciousness rather than category. Much like Molière's bourgeois gentleman who, when told about the distinction between prose and poetry, exclaimed '*Par ma foi, il y a plus de quarante ans que je dis de la prose, sans que j'en susse rien*' ('Good lord, for over forty years I have been speaking prose and I did not know it'), the exponents of the new tongue in that era would be shocked to hear that they were speaking a different language, one whose name would eventually be linked to military barracks (*orda* in Turkish).

Like all languages, Urdu emerged into consciousness primarily as speech and song, and did not detach itself from its roots in Hindavi grammar, Turkish/Pali vocabularies and plebeian deployment (as opposed to scriptural Sanskrit or courtly Persian) until the taxonomies of colonialism ripped it apart from Devanagri. If one is looking for a definite date when Urdu was born, one should consider the year 1900, in which Anthony MacDonnell's infamous 'Nagri resolution' postulated that Hindi and Urdu were separate languages. But to do that would get us ahead of our story. For the moment, imagine if you will, a new way of speaking, that emerged as a fad and began spreading like wildfire across northern and western India, adopted by Sufi mendicants, bhakti singers, street balladeers and regular working folk who did not have access to more courtly languages. Imagine tradespeople, holy men and other travellers who seeded the countryside with its common metaphors, turns of phrase and grammatical peculiarities. The argot grew in usage and popularity, flying under the radar of Persian court records, classical poems in Sanskrit, and florid Turkish tracts.

Then came Mir.

It is difficult to understate the role played by Mir Taqi Mir in legitimizing Urdu as a language of culture as well as popular communication in the eighteenth century. I do not intend to offer biographical sketches of any poets in this introduction; I do that when I introduce their poems. But Mir was not just a person; he was also a phenomenon, a force of Urdu nature. It was he who provided innovative rhyme schemes, metaphoric codes and subject matter—a roadmap that future poets could adopt. His contemporaries like Mirza Sauda and Khwaja Dard in Delhi were able to leverage that insight into the building blocks of a tradition. Parallel movements in other parts of north India contributed to the emergence of a relatively unselfconscious mode of poetic and literary expression in the new argot. The Mir era may have been the moment when Urdu began to achieve legitimacy, when the stuffed *Farsi-daan*s of the Mughal court realized that this argot that had become the lingua franca of the subaltern class actually had poetic potential that far exceeded the derivative Persian of the court tracts, the ghostwritten princely memoirs or even the classical *mushaira*s (social gatherings where poets gathered to recite poetry, often in the form of a contest). The ghazal in the hands of Mir became a rapier, touching the vulnerable part of the listener's heart in a way Hafiz may have touched the Persian heart, but which no Indian had replicated in Farsi. Mind you, the language was still known primarily as Rekhti, though 'Urdu' was now becoming an accepted word as well. Mir's acolytes adhered faithfully to the guidelines set by his creative genius, producing what we now refer to as the 'Delhi school' of Urdu poetry. Outside of Delhi, there were stalwarts like Nazeer Akbarabadi writing the era's equivalent of top hits in the *nazm* tradition, and parallel developments in the prose world led to the emergence of a loose consensus around how the language would be scripted.

A brief but vital digression into the Urdu prose tradition is necessary here. Until the eighteenth century, traditions of Urdu prose had been overwhelmingly oral, relying on the narrative powers of *dastan*s (epics) such as *Char Darvesh, Hatim Tai, Betal Pachchisi, Gul-e Bakawali, Laila Majnun, Panchatantra* and others. Also influential were the traditions that were derived from the folklore associated with the Islamic Empire, such as the dastan of Amir Hamza. Enter the famous press started by Munshi Nawal Kishore in Lucknow in 1858. This press began to tap into a vast market, which had been starved of popular fiction. One of the best-known offerings of Nawal Kishore Press, Pandit Ratan Nath Sarshar's *Fasana-e Aazad* (The Legend of Aazad), is often spoken of as Urdu's first novel. Somewhat similar in structure to *Don Quixote*, *Fasana-e Aazad* chronicles the travels of a modernist nobleman Azad, and his reluctant rustic companion, Khoji, who embarks on a series of adventures to win the hand of a beautiful woman named Husn-Ara. The journey of Urdu fiction from *Fasana-e Aazad* to Mirza Rusva's *Umrao Jaan Ada*, and then on to Premchand's *Godaan*, and eventually Qurratulain Hyder's *Aag ka Darya* is fascinating, which we shall reluctantly set aside in order to return to poetry.

A parallel movement in the eighteenth century was the maturing of the *marsiya* tradition, especially in Lucknow. The religious observances of Shia Muslims during the month of Mohurrum have always involved poetic representations of the events surrounding the battle of Karbala where Imam Husain, the grandson of Prophet Mohammed, was martyred. The Karbala passion play has provided a fertile ground for poets in a variety of languages. Urdu was no exception, but thanks to the extraordinary literary ability of the eighteenth-century marsiya poets, in particular Mir Anees and Mirza Dabeer, the marsiya or elegy emerged as a robust literary form in its own right, a tradition that endures till today.

After Mir, came Ghalib.

Like Mir, Ghalib is not just a personage in the history of Urdu poetry but an era. The Ghalib stage in the nineteenth century arguably represented an apotheosis of sorts for Urdu *sukhan*, or the poetic aesthetic. Asadullah Khan Ghalib (known lovingly among Urduwalas as *chacha* Ghalib, and to Hyderabadis simply as *chicha*) took the poets of his era who were still recycling Mir's tropes to school with his incredible riffs on philosophy and love and politics, making it clear who the real inheritor of Mir's mantle was. Despite his poverty, cantankerous nature and needless obsession with Persian (which led him to devalue his own Urdu poetry and waste time on inferior Farsi efforts), he was recognized as a genius in his own time (at least by the cognoscenti), and in the 150 years since his death he has acquired the status of a colossus in the poetic landscape of Urdu. The *Deevan-e Ghalib* may be the most highly printed book in the history of Urdu literature, and Ghalib's verse may be the most translated.

While Ghalib was producing his magic in Delhi, the Deccan was displaying its own brand of renaissance. The rulers of Hyderabad were courting artistes like Zauq in much the same way a current IPL franchise may court an upcoming player. Zauq's regretful rejection was communicated to the Hyderabadis poetically, and gave the Delhi-ites a sher with which to gloat forever:

In dinon gar-che Dakkan mein hai badi qadr-e sukhan
Kaun jaaye Zauq par Dilli ki galiyaan chhod kar

Although in the Deccan they value poetry these days
O Zauq, who can forsake Delhi's wondrous lanes and byways?

Dagh Dehlavi, a future exponent of the Zauq–Ghalib style of poetry, would eventually move to Hyderabad, where mushairas in the nineteenth century occupied the cultural space that an A.R. Rahman concert might in the early twenty-first century. Poetry began to be published in journals and magazines, newspapers regularly carried ghazals, nazms and literary criticism, and an indigenous movement produced what would become the foundation of an Urdu literary tradition.

Moreover, the Fort William College was founded in Calcutta in the early nineteenth century. Admittedly a colonial institution designed to help the British rule India better, the college (along with its counterpart, the Delhi College) produced a variety of translations of Urdu tracts, exposed Urdu to Western literature through commissioned translations, and produced a corpus of knowledge that, despite its imperial motivations, helped the language immeasurably in broadening its offerings.

The momentum gained by Urdu in the nineteenth century was however to be rudely interrupted by the 1857 war of independence. The savagery with which the British put down the 'mutiny' as they called it was unparalleled. In northern India, the entire princely system was dismantled; court patronage shrivelled for those who depended on the nawabs and rajas for their stipends. While Urdu flourished a bit more in the southern parts of the country where the effects of the post-1857 repression were less overt, the renaissance of Urdu suffered a body blow in the late nineteenth century.

As officialized Urdu began to be viewed with great suspicion, it generated an interesting phase of introspection and, in my opinion, defensiveness. The Urdu intellectuals of that time were forced to evaluate—and at times even benchmark—their work against that of their new masters, and Urdu poetry and literary criticism of the late nineteenth century reflects this artificial and stylized engagement with Western poetic and literary convention. Critics such as Sir Sayyid Ahmad Khan, Mohammad Husain Azad, Altaf Husain Hali and Shibli Nomani wrote defensively about their language, vacillating between advocations of modernity and a retreat into religiosity. Sir Sayyid of course is best known for the foundation of the Muhammadan Anglo-Oriental College in 1875, which later became the Aligarh Muslim University, the bastion of modernist pedagogy in the nineteenth and twentieth centuries. Mohammad Husain Azad wrote *Aab-e Hayaat* (Water of Life) in 1880, arguably the first comprehensive work of Urdu literary criticism, in which he made evocative pleas for Urdu poets to embrace natural themes, in keeping with the Western (British) literary mores of his time. In effect he was asking them to dial down the metaphysics. Altaf Husain Hali had made a similar invocation in 1893 when, in his *Muqaddama-e Sher-o-Shairi* (Exegesis on Poems and Poetry), he decried the Urdu poetry of his time as excessively metaphor-driven, and argued for a more naturalistic approach. Ironically, he had himself not shied from the use of florid metaphors while composing his famous *musaddas*, a long epic poem lamenting the decay of morals in the Islamic world.

By the early twentieth century, the aforementioned Anthony MacDonnell—who enacted the implicit British policy of

intensifying existing Hindu–Muslim tensions to help them
govern the colony with greater ease—injected language into the
communal debate. In 1900, he passed the 'Nagri Resolution',
which produced an artificial taxonomic schism between Urdu
and Hindi, thereby separating the languages according to
religious affiliation. Communalists on both sides of the religious
divide rejoiced, but others were less sanguine. Mohsin-ul Mulk,
a prominent poet-politician of the time, saw it as the beginning
of the demise of Urdu, and wrote an elegy to it in the form of
a couplet:

Chal saath, ke hasrat dil-e mahroom se nikle
Aashiq ka janaaza hai, zara dhoom se nikle

Walk along with that heartbroken procession awhile
It's the funeral of a lover, bury him in style.

In the post–World War I era, Urdu seemed destined to
be seen as a language of Muslims, a mantle that was almost
comically at odds with its multi-religious origins. It is in this
era of ambivalence that we must place Allama Mohammed
Iqbal, a genius who straddled the divide between the traditions
of the East and the modernist renaissance of the West. Iqbal it
was who first spoke of modernist notions like selfhood (*khudi*),
hitherto absent in Urdu poetry. The battle between free will
and determinism, according to Iqbal, was really one the human
could control:

Khudi ko kar buland itna, ke har taqdeer se pehle
Khuda bande se khud poochhe, bataa teri raza kya hai?

Exalt your Self thus, that before every twist of fate
God should say, 'My creation, on your desire I wait.'

Iqbal flirted with the ultimate act of iconoclasm, casting
Lucifer (*Iblees*) as a tragic hero. He produced imaginary
conversations between God and Lenin. And it was he who, in his
epic 1909 poem *Shikva* (Complaint), elevated the human being
to the status of a petitioner who commented critically on God's
act of creation. While Iqbal's poetry can be seen as a reflection
on the state of Islam and of Muslims as they prepared to engage
with modernity, it carried (in my opinion) less of the conservative
angst of Hali and more of a globalized sentiment, as he strove to
connect the experiences of South Asians with their counterparts
in Central Asia, Europe and the Middle East, and envisioned
a more creative engagement between 'religions', be they Islam,
Hinduism, Christianity, modernism, or Marxism.

In the mid-twentieth century, Urdu was to receive a gift
that would revive it in spectacular fashion as a language of
revolution and hope, of social change and religious heresy, as a
symbol of the human will to be free and as the defiant enemy of
divisiveness. I am referring to the 'progressive phase' in which
Urdu writers (and especially Urdu poets) became the vanguard
of a literary movement that combined socialism, anti-colonial
sentiment, inter-religious harmony, the foundation of a new
nationalism, gender equality, and an ethos of a shared literary
and political heritage across all Indian languages and indeed
across the globe.[4] The broader community of progressive poets
included non-Urdu stalwarts such as Sumitranandan Pant and
Maithilisharan Gupt (Hindi), Rabindranath Tagore (Bengali),
Sri Sri (Telugu), Umashankar Joshi (Gujarati), Gurbaksh Singh
(Punjabi) and Anna Bhau Sathe (Marathi). Hasrat Mohani, Josh
Malihabadi, Firaaq Gorakhpuri, Makhdoom Mohiuddin, Sahir
Ludhianvi, Faiz Ahmed Faiz, Asrar-ul Haq Majaz, Ali Sardar
Jafri, Jan Nisar Akhtar, Kaifi Azmi and others commandeered
Urdu poetry for well over four decades, producing works that
drastically altered the conventions of poetic content, while

hewing true (for the most part) to the classical form. Josh summed up their agenda pithily:

Kaam hai mera taghayyur, naam mera hai shabaab
Mera naara inquilaab-o inquilaab-o inquilaab

My name is youth, and upheaval is my mission
My slogan: Revolution. Revolution. Revolution.

The Progressive Writers' Association, which was formed in 1936, became the conduit through which a variety of poets expressed ideas that challenged the socio-cultural status quo and provided the real possibility of taking the freedom movement in the subcontinent in the direction of social justice.

Contemporary with the progressive movement (*taraqqi pasand tehreek*) were the purveyors of modernism (*jadeediyat*) who preferred to experiment with form more than content. The mutual contempt that the progressives and modernists had for each other was perhaps unfortunate, for it precluded interesting conversational possibilities between them. However, the work of modernist poets like Noon Meem Rashid, Miraji and the members of the *Halqa-e Arbaab-e Zauq* (circle of connoisseurs) has stood the test of time. Perhaps their greater contribution has been to rescue Urdu poetry from the prison of metre (*zameen*) that it had always found itself in. Jazz-like improvisations abound in the poetry of Rashid in particular, where non-linear narratives mix with layered thoughts, with the poet gleefully 'contaminating' conscious feelings and unconscious desires in a palimpsest of literary production.

The freedom movement also produced a frenzy of activity among the Urdu poets in the 1930s and 1940s. I remember my late father, who was nineteen when India achieved its freedom, declaim poems from memory that I have never seen in print (and for all I know, he never read either, but rather imbibed orally). One of them bears repeating, for it demonstrates simplicity and songlike rhythm. It was a taunt directed at a well-dressed Englishman, invoking an old Urdu term that referred to disloyal people as 'white-blooded':

Ye coat bhi sufaid, ye patloon bhi sufaid
Teri sufaid hat ka hai oon bhi sufaid
Khud jism bhi sufaid hai, aur is ke saath saath
Main to ye jaanta hoon, tera khoon bhi sufaid

White is your coat and white your pants flat
As is the white wool on your white hat
Your body is white and I do know that
Your blood is white, you betrayer rat.

Literary critics might think such verse doggerel, but when situated in its milieu, it carries the resonance, meaning and anger of a population that was ready to set itself free from the yoke of foreigners. As the mid 1940s appeared, the Urdu poets of that generation sharpened their quills and began to ready themselves to write panegyrics to the newborn nation.

However, just as 1857 had once snuffed out the renaissance of Urdu poetry, 1947 was another catastrophic moment. The dawn of independence brought with it not the red horizon of a new day, but a horizon reddened with the blood of Partition. Like the last gasp of a dying taper, poets wrote expressive poems about their grief at the moment their hopes were betrayed. In Faiz's words: '*Vo intezaar tha jis ka, ye vo sahar to nahin*' ('This is not the dawn that we had awaited'). Or in Josh's grieving hyperbole: '*Apna gala kharosh-e tarannum se phat gayaa / Talvaar se bachaa, to rag-e gul se kat gayaa*' ('Our throat was torn by a song sharp as a stinging nettle / It evaded the sword, but was slit by a rose petal').

The Partition geographically divided a poetic fraternity, and produced different tensions on both sides of the border. While the Urduwalas on the Indian side had to contend with a new regime of suspicion and intolerance, the Pakistani poets (especially the progressives) faced persecution by the elite class for advocating social change and wealth redistribution. The wars between India and Pakistan, the decline of social patronage, the inability to replicate the critical mass of readers and enthusiasts, combined with the general disappointment of the failed promise of decolonization, freedom and nationalism, led to another wasted opportunity for Urdu.

But like the survivor it always was, Urdu found itself a new champion in India—in the film industry.[5] The language of what is popularly known as Hindi cinema has always been friendly to Urdu expression. The producers of Indian cinema commissioned songs by Urdu poets, thereby not only providing them with livelihood opportunities, but also serving to keep Urdu idioms alive in popular usage. When Javed Akhtar uses Persianized phrases like '*Aql-o-hosh nameedanam*' ('Wisdom and consciousness are lost') before exhorting the 'hot girls' to put their hands up and the 'cool boys' to make some noise in the 2007 film *Om Shanti Om*, he is participating in a longer tradition, where the rhythms of popular culture have been infiltrated by Urdu. This tradition of course dates back well over fifty years. For instance, while Sahir Ludhianvi was composing urgent political poems like his anti-war opus *Parchhaiyan* (Silhouettes) in the 1950s, he was also getting Johnny Walker in the 1957 film *Pyaasa* to suggest:

Sar jo tera chakraaye, ya dil dooba jaaye,
Aaja pyare paas hamaare, kaahe ghabraae, kaahe ghabraae

If your head spins, or your heart sinks, my dear
Come to me [have a massage], why fear, why fear?

Hindi movies have used classical Urdu poems in set situations; we may remember Deepak Parashar pining for Salma Agha in the 1982 film *Nikaah* while Ghulam Ali belted out '*Chupke chupke raat din aansoo bahaana yaad hai*' ('Nights and days of quiet tear-shedding, I still remember') from a ghazal, written originally by Hasrat Mohani a century ago. Likewise, the cognoscenti may recall the 1963 film *Gumraah* where a dashing Sunil Dutt sits at the piano and suggests to Sadhana, '*Chalo ek baar phir se ajnabi ban jaayen hum dono*' ('Come, let us become strangers again'), B.R. Chopra having reworked a previously published and already famous nazm by Sahir Ludhianvi into its narrative. More importantly, Urdu poets like Sahir, Majrooh, Kaifi, Shakeel Badayuni and others were able to infuse the idiomatic conventions of classical Urdu poetry into popular consciousness, a task that Javed Akhtar and Gulzar continue admirably today. Film music also led the way for an explosion of non-filmi music, where Urdu poetry also found representation and a place for international crossover. Pakistani singers like Ghulam Ali, Mehdi Hasan, Abida Parveen, Nusrat Fateh Ali Khan, the Sabri Brothers, Iqbal Bano, Nayyara Noor and a host of others became household names in India, competing with such local stalwarts as Jagjit Singh, Panjak Udhas and others.

Two other movements deserve mention. In the 1960s, several Urdu poets, whose aesthetic inclinations were linked to the aforementioned Halqa-e Arbaab-e Zauq, intensified the infusion of modernist metaphor in Urdu poetry. Their efforts were championed by the literary journal *Shabkhoon* (Night Attack), under the stewardship of Shamsur Rahman Faruqi, and in Pakistan by journals such as *Auraq* (Pages) edited by Dr Wazir Agha. The neo-modern wave in Urdu poetry fostered a conscious union between the craft of the poet and the self-conscious language of the literary critic. The traditions of jadeediyat were strengthened, poets felt free to use free verse (*aazad nazm*) rather than the constricting boundaries of rhyme and metre, and the symbols of personal metaphysics were valued over the collectivist ethos of progressivism. Across the Atlantic, academics in the US supported these movements through journals such as *Mahfil* and the *Annual of Urdu Studies*. It was through the support of such institutions that the postmodernist turn also reached Urdu literature, where the weariness with the metanarratives of progressivism produced poems that shrugged off the imperatives of representation, and crafted an uber-personal literary ethos.

In a rather different vein, in the southern part of the subcontinent, poets from the Dakkani tradition like Sulaiman Khateeb and Sarwar Danda produced exquisite social commentaries through humorous poetry (*mazaahiya shaayiri*) that expressed through irony and wistfulness those sentiments that might have shattered the heart if spoken of directly. Protagonists of this craft in the Deccan—like Siraj Nirmali, Paagal Adilabadi, Himayatullah and Mujtaba Husain—deserve place in the Urdu canon. Their defiantly plebeian aesthetic[6] connected with their audience (for theirs was first and foremost an oral tradition), and perhaps struck a middle road between the programmatic socialism of the progressives and the self-absorbed ruminations of the modernists. It is a tragic matter that the canon, which is conditioned to view aesthetic experimentation with simplicity as aesthetic failure, was never able to value the Dakkani humorists in its conventional scale.[7]

Discerning readers who have come thus far in the narrative may notice a significant omission—not a single woman poet has been mentioned in the discussion yet. Was there a paucity of women poets writing Urdu poetry all these years? Were they of inferior quality compared to the masters mentioned thus far? I am inclined to answer both questions with an emphatic no, but the reality is that the work of women poets in the seventeenth–eighteenth centuries has been under-represented, and is difficult to find. To the extent that I have not made extra efforts to find it, I acknowledge my intellectual laziness, and promise to redress this in future offerings. I had heard of the poet Saeedunnisa Hirma, who wrote in the nineteenth century, but her work has been tough to locate. Also, as a Hyderabadi, I had heard of the eighteenth-century courtesan poet Mahlaqa Bai 'Chanda' (1767–1824), who not only wrote poetry (her Persian *deevan* was published in 1797 and a posthumous Urdu collection appeared in the mid-nineteenth century), but was a patron of the arts, and sustained several poets. Zahida Khatoon Shervani, another Dakkani poet, wrote *Aaeena-e Haram*, a collection of poems, in 1927. I am also acquainted with *Baharistan-e Naz*, a collection of Urdu poetry by women, and plan to do some justice to this aspect and fill the gaping hole in my own understanding as well as the representation of women poets in classical Urdu poetry in future work. I will settle now for an apology and a promise to correct the gender imbalance in my account of Urdu poetry.[8] Happily, I have been able to include a variety of twentieth-century Urdu women poets in this collection, many of whom write bravely and eloquently not just about love and romance but also about patriarchy, oppression and political engagement in a way that enhances our understanding of current social and political challenges and represents the best that Urdu poetry has to offer today.

Urdu continues to be a vibrant and lively language. With the advent of the Internet, we see a proliferation of Urdu websites, of video recordings of mushairas and songs, and of the dissemination of scholarly work. The web continues to build bridges connecting the archipelago that constituted scholarly work in Urdu. Also, researchers have now begun to compile and catalogue its impressive corpus of literature and research; for instance, recently, Anwar Moazzam and Ashhar Farhan of Hyderabad have compiled a bibliography of social science research in Urdu[9]. Every day new books are published on Urdu poetry, including criticism, anthologies and collections. The language continues to struggle with religious orthodoxy, and many current debates underscore its conflicted relationship with the mosque and its affinity for the street. Urdu remains the language of the present, and by way of showcasing its cosmopolitan and its contemporary ethos, I'd like to offer a poem by Lata Haya, a poet of remarkable performative ability I encountered only through the Internet, and whose poem here congratulates Urdu on the advent of the new millennium:

Subh ka pehla payaam, Urdu
Dhalti hui se jaise sham, Urdu
Utrey jo taare wahi baam, Urdu
Badi kamsin gulfaam, Urdu
Jaise naye saal ka ye din ho naya
Aur beetey saal ki ho aakhri dua
Naya saal, nayi Ram Ram, Urdu
Tujhe nayi sadi ka salaam Urdu

The first message of the dawn, Urdu
Like the slowly setting sun, Urdu
Where the stars descend, that roof, Urdu
A youthful beauty you are, Urdu
Like the new day of the New Year
And the last blessing of the old one
Happy New Year, and a new hello, Urdu
The new century salutes you, Urdu.

To some, the twenty-first century represents the dying gasps of Urdu poetry. But to those pessimists, may I say that the rumours of Urdu's demise have been exaggerated for well over 150 years. Urdu was on the verge of death in 1857 (post 'mutiny'), 1901 (post 'Nagri resolution'), 1947 (post-Partition), 1951 (when the Uttar Pradesh Official Language Act derecognized Urdu), and 2001 (post–9/11, for reasons not very clear, beyond the fact that everyone wants to associate that date with everything). However, as long as a chill runs up your spine when you hear a verse by Ghalib, as long as marchers on the street shout '*Inquilab Zindabad*', and as long as film lyricists like Gulzar compose lines like '*Woh yaar hai jo khushboo ki tarah / Jis ki zuban Urdu ki tarah*' ('It is a friend who appears like fragrance / And whose language is [sweet] like Urdu'), we have no problem. I am counting on my great-great-grandchildren wringing their hands and lamenting the eventual demise of Urdu in 2150. And I won't be surprised if the language continues to prevail nevertheless, for Urdu poetry is, after all, written by angels. In Chicha's words:

Aate hain ghaib se ye mazaameen khayaal mein
Ghalib, sareer-e khaama navaa-e sarosh hai

These rare ideas I dare invent
A zephyr from paradise brings,
Ghalib's sounds of pen on parchment
Are the flutter of angel wings.

A NOTE ON POETIC FORM

Mir Anees, the great marsiya poet, and arguably one of the finest exponents of the art of Urdu poetry, was reputed to have composed his first sher when he was a child of five. Having watched his pet goat die, he apparently ran weeping to his father and said:

Afsos ke duniya se safar kar gayi bakri
Aankhen to khuli reh gaeen, par mar gayi bakri

Alas the goat's soul departed for heaven
It is truly dead, though the goat's eyes are open

I am struck by the rhythmic quality of this couplet, fashioned so beautifully by the young Anees. The tyke seems to have had perfect rhyme and metre from the start, and as he grew older, content must have fed technique in a harmonious cycle that peaked in his extraordinary prowess, where the most complex of emotions and situations were rendered in metred verse with not an ounce of effort showing. Such are the ways in which the poets of Urdu sharpened their technique—through countless repetitions of poems, a craft practised over and over again, tested in the furnace of mushairas, where jealous contemporaries and, occasionally, gentle teachers separated the wheat from the chaff. It was not enough to be solely an exponent of form or a purveyor of content in those rarefied circles. One needed to be both.

Over time, as poets tested their craft among peers and the listening public, a protocol of sorts emerged regarding the form poetry would take. Much like the way Indian classical musicians were trained within the boundaries of specific ragas, Urdu poets learned the protocols of the ghazal and other poetic forms, which they either adhered to or tweaked. Here, I briefly discuss five forms that are relatively common in Urdu poetry, namely the ghazal, the *qataa*, the *rubaai*, the musaddas, and the nazm (along with its variant, the aazad nazm). I should say at the outset that such a discussion of poetic conventions need not necessarily get between the reader and the enjoyment of poetry (just as you do not need to know the difference between a backward short leg and a leg slip to enjoy cricket). But such nuances are nonetheless interesting to know.

GHAZAL

The ghazal is the dominant form of the Urdu poem. It is structured relatively strictly, with a string of shers (couplets), common in metre (i.e. the first and second lines have the same number of syllables). Every second line of a couplet in a ghazal shares a rhythmic continuity with every other second line, through two artefacts known as the *qafiya* and the *radif*. The qafiya primarily refers to a convention of using certain rhyming words in the course of a verse. The radif is the refrain at the end of a certain line that gives the verse a consistent rhythm.

To explain these in concrete terms, let us take an example of three shers from a popular ghazal, such as Hasrat Mohani's ghazal '*Chupke chupke*', which was used in the 1982 film *Nikaah*. The lines go thus:

> *Chupke chupke raat din aansoo bahaana yaad hai*
> *Hum ko ab tak aashiqui ka vo zamaana yaad hai*
> *Khainch lena vo mera parde ka kona daf'atan*
> *Aur dupatte mein tera vo moonh chhupaana yaad hai*
> *Dopahar ki dhoop mein mere bulaane ke liye*
> *Vo tera kothe pe nange paaon aana yaad hai*

> Nights, days of quiet tear-shedding, I still remember
> That era of intense loving, I still remember
> Suddenly, I pulled away the curtain between us
> Your veiled face playfully hiding, I still remember
> The afternoon sun, the hot roof, your bare, burning feet
> That sweet summons, you arriving, I still remember.

The rhyme in this ghazal derives primarily from the qafiya, which in this case comes from the rhyming of '*bahaana*', '*zamaana*', '*chhupaana*' and '*aana*'. It is here that the creativity of the poet is tested the most. The radif in this ghazal is '*yaad hai*', which is a base on which the ghazal stands. In this case, every second line of every stanza would end with the words '*yaad hai*' (the radif), and that phrase would be preceded by a word that rhymed with '*bahaana*' (the qafiya). Ghazals typically contain between five and twenty couplets, which are not necessarily connected to each other in narrative continuity.

Two more elements of the ghazal to keep in mind are the *matla* and the *maqta*. The matla is a sher in the ghazal, usually the first couplet, where both lines rhyme. The first sher in the above ghazal is a matla. A ghazal may have more than one matla; for instance, in the Faiz ghazal '*Tum aaye ho*' that I have translated in this volume, the first two shers are both considered matlas. The maqta is that sher of a ghazal which contains the poet's name as a signature (the signature is known as the *takhallus*). Many of the ghazals in this anthology have maqtas, which are often the place where poets showed their flourish. Often, a poet may have more than one takhallus. Ghalib had two: 'Ghalib' and, occasionally, 'Asad'. As he said:

> *Main ne Majnun pe ladakpan mein, Asad*
> *Sang uthaya thha, ke sar yaad aaya*

> In my childhood, Asad
> I raised a stone to strike Majnu dead
> But then,
> I remembered my own head.

Typically, the maqta is the last sher of the ghazal. But poets may choose to tweak the format. For example, in the ghazal '*Insha-ji utho*' translated in this book, the matla and the maqta are the same sher.

QATAA

A qataa, very simply, is a poem of four lines—a quatrain. It may occur in the middle of a ghazal (where the poet is unable to finish a thought in two lines, and chooses to use four). It may also be a stand-alone verse, un-embedded in any long poem. Here is an example of a stand-alone qataa from Faiz:

> *Raat yoon dil mein teri khoi hui yaad aayi*
> *Jaise veerane mein chupke se bahaar aa jaaye*
> *Jaise sehraaon mein haule se chale baad-e naseem*
> *Jaise beemar ko be-vajah qaraar aa jaaye*

Your faded memory visited my heart last night
As if the spring came to the ruins, real quiet
As if the zephyr silently cooled the desert
And the sick, miraculously, gained some respite.

RUBAAI

Like a qataa, a rubaai is a four-liner, but it is always a stand-alone mini-poem in its own right. Its rhyming scheme is fixed, with the first, second and fourth line rhyming, while the third line is free. In this sense, one can say that all rubaais are also qataas but all qataas are not rubaais. Furthermore, an astute observer may ask if there is indeed a subtle difference between a stand-alone qataa that follows this fixed rhyme scheme, and a rubaai. The answer really appears to lie in an additional requirement, that the verses of the rubaai should have twelve syllables, and must be amenable to a certain kind of intonation.

Rubaais were very popular in Farsi poetry (with Omar Khayyam's poems crossing the linguistic divide into English). One of the best-regarded exponents of the rubaai was Josh Malihabadi; this is considered one of his best:

Ghunche, teri be-basi pe dil hilta hai
Tu ek tabassum ke liye khilta hai
Ghunche ne kaha ke is chaman mein baba
Ye ek tabassum bhi kise milta hai

Dear flower, my heart does shake at your sorry plight
For one smile from your love does your blossom take flight!
The flower said, 'Dear friend, don't mock this garden's grace
One smile I have. That's more than other creatures might.'

MUSADDAS

A musaddas may be simply described as a poem in which each unit consists of six lines. Typically, the first four lines of the musaddas rhyme with each other, while the last two rhyme in a different format. This poetic form lends itself to longer narratives and epic poems, and has been adopted especially by purveyors of the marsiya (an elegy that usually describes events surrounding an important event in Islamic history—the battle of Karbala). Mir Anees and Mirza Dabeer are prominent exponents of the marsiya tradition. Of the non-marsiya poems, the musaddas by Maulana Altaf Husain Hali is popular, as are Iqbal's two long poems, *Shikva* and *Jawaab-e Shikva*. A typical musaddas may have over a hundred six-line verses.

Here, I present a verse from a marsiya by Mir Anees, which is a good exemplar of the musaddas with clean rhythms and evocative *manzar-kashi*, or the ability of the poet to depict a scene as drama. This verse describes the moment before Imam Husain leaves for his final battle. The menfolk have all perished; he is in the company of only his little daughter Sakina and his sister Bibi Zainab. This particular verse is one of the most celebrated marsiya verses, having been performed repeatedly in the public domain as well as featured in Shyam Benegal's *Sardari Begum* (1996).

Husain jab ke chale baad-e dopahar ran ko
Na thha koi ke jo thhaame rakaab-e tausan ko
Sakina jhaad rahi thhi abaa ke daaman ko
Husain chup ke khade thhe jhukaaye gardan ko
Na aasra thha koi shah-e karbalaai ko
Faqat savaar kiya thha bahan ne bhai ko

That fateful afternoon, ready to fight stood brave Husain
No one to help him mount his horse, loneliness fed his pain
Little Sakina brushed his robe, her sadness to contain
Husain simply stood with head bowed, and quietude did reign
Karbala's hero was alone, no friends left to pay heed
His brave sister then stepped up, to help him mount his steed.

One could speak of other categories where longer poems have been done in specific rhyme schemes, like the *mukhammas*, a nazm with a five-line scheme (as in Nazeer Akbarabadi's '*Aadmi-Nama*' in this volume).

NAZM

Nazm translates to mean 'poem', and in that sense, every poem is a nazm. However, in ordinary usage, nazm refers to that poem which does not fall into any specific rhythmic category. Typically, the nazm is associated with narrative continuity, that is, it tells a single story, unlike the syncopated content of the ghazal. It is also longer than the qataa or the rubaai, and does not follow the stringent structural demands of a musaddas. Many of the works of Sahir, Faiz, Majaz and others in this anthology, come under the nazm category.

The aazad nazm is nothing more than a nazm liberated from the conventions of metre, and often, rhyme. The works of Noon Meem Rashid, Javed Akhtar and Gulzar in this volume are exemplars of the aazad nazm. Free verse in Urdu, however, retains still a lot more rhythm than a free verse poem in English or other European languages.

OTHER CATEGORIZATIONS AND TERMS

One may choose to categorize poems according to content rather than form, in which case a poem might be seen as a *naat* (a religious poem in praise of Prophet Mohammed), a *hamd* (a poem in praise of Allah), a *qaseeda* (a poem in praise of some person or being other than these two entities), or, as noted earlier, a marsiya (an elegy). One could speak of a poem according to performance, such as a qawwali, which is a group song with specific repetitive manoeuvres. For a delightful example of a performed qawwali, watch the Sabri Brothers perform '*Saqiya aur pila*' ('Some more wine please, cupbearer') on YouTube.

Another term one hears about a lot is a *deevan*. A deevan is an anthology of a poet's work, but usually contains only ghazals. The ghazals are ordered according to the last letter of the ghazal, and the deevan must contain ghazals that end with at least each letter of the Urdu alphabet. So the smallest possible deevan will have around twenty-five poems. Usually, they are much larger; for instance Ghalib's deevan has 234 poems.

I hope the reader is not daunted by these terms and categories. Like I've mentioned earlier, discussions of poetic form should be considered secondary to the enjoyment of a poem's rhythms. Onwards then, to the poets and poems themselves.

POEMS

AMIR KHUSRAU

Amir Khusrau (1253–1325), the thirteenth-century maestro, is associated with Persian literature as well as the qawwali form of Sufi mystical poetry, but his forays into the Urdu/Hindavi tradition find him at his playful best. His popular qawwalis like '*Zehaal-e miskin nakun taghaaful*' ('Do not ignore the plight of the poverty-stricken') are pure Persian, and exhibit immense gravitas. By contrast, one of the best-known Urdu/Hindavi poems, '*Chhap tilak sab chheeni re mosay naina milaike*' ('You have stolen my looks merely by gazing into my eyes') is much more lyrically light, and has been performed repeatedly for more than 700 years.

In this anthology, I have chosen to highlight that aspect of Khusrau's work which not only straddles the spurious Hindi–Urdu divide but also brings out the light-hearted quality of his poetic personality, one that puts him in the company of authors such as Lewis Carroll or Sukumar Ray.[1] I translate below a few of Khusrau's riddle poems and a qawwali. In contemporary culture, this qawwali ('*Chhap tilak*') features often as a song in movies: for instance, in the 1978 film *Main Tulsi Tere Aangan ki*. It has been performed by a variety of singers including Sabri Brothers, Nusrat Fateh Ali Khan, Richa Sharma and—my favourite—Abida Parveen. Note how the poet affects a feminine first person, and expresses affection for a male beloved ('Nijaam' here refers to Nizamuddin Auliya, the dear companion of Khusrau).

1   **DO-SUKHNE (DOUBLE ENTENDRES)**

These are specific riddles, where two questions lead to the same answer, made possible by deploying a word in the answer that has two meanings.

> *Deevar kyoon tooti?*
> *Rah kyoon luti?*
> *Raj na tha.*

> Why did the wall fall, won't you say?
> What made life unsafe on the highway?
> There was no mason/There was no governance.

*

> *Ghar kyon andhiyara?*
> *Faqeer kyon badbadaya?*
> *Diya na tha.*

> Why does the house languish in the dark?
> Why did the beggar angrily bark?
> There was no lamp/Nothing was given.

*

> *Raja pyasa kyoon?*
> *Gadha udasa kyoon?*
> *Lota na tha.*

> Why was the king thirsty, my lad?
> And why did the donkey appear so sad?
> There was no tumbler/He had not rolled in the mud.

2   PAHELIYAAN (RIDDLES)

Many of Khusrau's riddles are structured so that the answer
lies within the text of the riddle itself.

> *Beeson ka sir kaat liya,*
> *Na maara na khoon kiya.*
> *Jawaab: Nakhoon*
> [Author's Note: *Na+khoon*]

I cut off twenty heads and still,
No blood did I shed, no one did I kill.
Answer: Nail (cutting).

*

> *Ek guni ne ye gun keena*
> *Hariyal pinjrey mein de deena*
> *Dekho jadoogar ka kamaal*
> *Daale hara, nikaale laal.*
> *Jawaab: Paan.*

A wise man did perform this feat
I'll cage this green parrot, he said
Observe the sorcerer; this trick is neat
In went the green and out came red!
Answer: The betel leaf (green before chewing, red after).

*

> *Ek naari ke sir par hai naar*
> *Pi ki lagan main khadi laachar*
> *Sees chuve aur chale na jor*
> *Ro ro kar woh kare hai bhor*
> *Jawaab: Mombatti*

Observe the woman with fire on her head
She burns as she awaits her beloved
Her body melts, her spirit mourns
And thus she suffers till the day dawns
Answer: Candle.

CHHAAP TILAK

Chhaap tilak, sab cheeni re mo-say naina milai-ke

Prem bhatee ka madhva pilai-ke
Matvali kar leeni re mo-say naina milai-ke

Gori gori baiyyaan, hari hari chudiyan
Baiyyaan pakad dhar leeni re mo-say naina milai-ke

Bal bal jaaoon main torey rang rajwa
Apni si kar leeni re mo-say naina milai-ke

Khusrau Nijaam ke bal bal jayyiye
Mohey suhaagan keeni re mo-say naina milai-ke

MY LOOKS, MY SELF

My looks, my self, you have stolen them
Merely by locking eyes with me.

That love potion you made me drink
Has me teetering on the brink
Merely by locking eyes with me.

You clasped the fair hands of your queen
Those hands encased in bangles green
Merely by locking eyes with me.

I offer myself to my prince
Let me in your colour rinse
Merely by locking eyes with me.

Khusrau, I give myself up to
My dear Nizaam with such pride
He has turned me with his love
Into a radiant, blushing bride
Merely by locking eyes with me.

QULI QUTUB SHAH

Quli Qutub Shah (d. 1612) was one of the more celebrated kings of the Deccan, ascending the throne of Golkonda at a young age, and often credited with founding the city of Hyderabad.[1] He is also known to have composed poems in Telugu, which was consistent with his ecumenical temperament. His language reflects a curious mix of linguistic influences, comprising a bit of Turkish, a bit of the local Pali-oriented dialect, some Arabic words, and a lot of Sanskrit as well.

The ghazal I have chosen to represent his work is relatively simple, but as can be seen, this pioneering work has helped establish the stylistic conventions of the ghazal that endure even today, such as the rhyme schemes and the trope of unattained love. This ghazal has been deployed often in popular culture, most notably in the poignant climax of Shyam Benegal's 1975 film *Nishant*. The enjoyment of the poem will be enhanced by listening simultaneously to Malika Pukhraaj's magical rendition.

PIYA BAAJ

> *Piya baaj pyala piya jaaye na*
> *Piya baaj ek til jiya jaye na*

Nahin ishq jis vo bada kood hai
Kadhi us se mil besiya jaye na

Kahe the piya bin saboori karoon
Kahaa jaaye lekin kiya jaye na

Qutub Shah na de mujh deevane ko pand
Deevane ko kuchh pand diya jaye naa

WITHOUT MY LOVE

I cannot quaff the goblet without my love.
Nor can I live a moment without my love.

Crude is the one who does not feel
Love's power
I just cannot stand such a heel
He's no lover.

'Be patient without your love, this moment too will
      pass'
Such counsel to follow is impossible, alas!

Qutub Shah, your guidance to the madman, although
      wise
Has no effect, for his love is beyond your advice.

WALI DAKKANI

Wali Ahmed Khan (1667–1707) was associated with Aurangabad and Hyderabad, but died in Gujarat. He practised his craft in the late seventeenth century, and was acknowledged as the master of the ghazal format and of the proto-Urdu poetic tradition by stalwarts such as Mir and Ghalib. Many see Wali as the point of origin of Urdu poetry, perhaps because he was the first to publish a deevan. Mohammad Husain Azad, the author of *Aab-e Hayaat*, seems to have thought so as well. Wali will always be remembered for his optimistic poetry—exemplified by the couplet '*Raah-e mazmoon-e taaza band nahin / Ta-qayaamat khula ha baab-e sukhan*' ('The road to new ideas is not closed / The door of poetry will remain open forever')—which presaged the emergence of a long-standing literary tradition. Unfortunately, his name has now become associated with tragedy; in March 2002, his tomb, which had been a prominent landmark in the city of Ahmedabad, was demolished, razed and paved over by the mobs that ravaged Gujarat in the post-Godhra conflagration.

The ghazal I have chosen here exemplifies his clean rhymes, his ability to move from the Dakkani idiom to the North Indian Rekhti, and his allegiance to the ghazal as poetic form. This ghazal has been performed by many singers, most notably by Iqbal Bano.

JISE ISHQ KA TEER KAARI LAGE

Jise ishq ka teer kaari lage
Use zindagi kyon na bhaari lage

Na chhode mohabbat dam-e marg lag
Jise yaar jaani so yaari lage

Na hoye use jag mein hargiz qaraar
Jise ishq ki beqaraari lage

Har ek waqt mujh aashiq-e paak ko
Pyaare teri baat pyaari lage

Wali ko kahe tu agar ek bachan
Raqibaan ke dil mein kataari lage

THE ONE WHO IS STRUCK BY CUPID'S DEADLY DART

Once you are struck by Cupid's deadly dart
You'll find life a heavy burden, dear heart

Those who have felt their lover's fragrant breath
Won't cease in the ways of love until their death

Solace will never dilute my passion
Love's impatient heat has left me ashen

My love's transparent, unblemished and clear
Each word of yours I find lovely, my dear

With your Wali, if you share but a word
His rivals writhe as if pierced by a sword!

MIRZA SAUDA

The eighteenth century marked the beginning of a prolonged renaissance in Urdu poetry, and was kicked off by the triumvirate of Sauda, Dard and Mir. Mirza Sauda (1713–81) was Mir Taqi Mir's contemporary, and one of the early exponents of what came to be called the 'Delhi School' of poetry. Mir's senior in age, he tends to be eclipsed by his more illustrious counterpart even though he made an invaluable contribution to the decentring of the hegemony of Farsi as sole crucible of classical poetry. His language tended to be more decorous than Mir's, still imbued with Persian rhetoric. He did write—in the fashion of poets of his time—a volume of Persian poetry, but was known principally for his Rekhti work, and also for his mischievous satires. His satires were often composed on the spot, derided those in power, and sometimes led to financial losses. One story goes thus: A rich man's son once approached Sauda in public to become a tutor. Sauda asked him to recite some of his verses. The expectant pupil recited some verses of high quality, which Sauda immediately recognized as plagiarized fare. Sauda asked the man, 'What is your takhallus?' Replied the young man, '*Ummeedwaar*' (hopeful). On the spot, Sauda declaimed: '*Hai faiz se kisi ke shajar unka baardaar / Is vaaste kiya hai takhallus "ummeedwaar"*' ('With another's labour, his tree is fruitful, / Perhaps this is why his nom de plume is "hopeful"').

38

The shamefaced youngster exited hastily; Sauda had won bragging rights, but lost a potential patron.

I have chosen a single haunting ghazal that, to my mind, exemplifies Sauda's serious work.[1] Unlike Mir's accessible rhythms, Sauda affected a style of verbal flourish, perhaps owing to his felicity in writing *qasida*s (panegyrics).

HUA SO HUA

> *Jo guzri mujh pe mat us se kaho hua so hua*
> *Balaa-kashaan-e mohabbat mein jo hua so hua*
>
> *Mubaadaa ho koi zaalim tera gireban-geer*
> *Mere lahu ko to daaman se dho, hua so hua*
>
> *Pahunch chukaa hai sar-e zakhm dil talak yaaro*
> *Koi siyo, koi marham karo hua so hua*
>
> *Kahe hai sun ke meri sar-guzasht vo be-rehm*
> *Ye kaun zikr hai, jaane bhi do, hua so hua*
>
> *Ye kaun haal hai ahvaal-e dil pe ai aankhon*
> *Na phoot phoot ke itna baho, hua so hua*
>
> *Diya use dil-o-zeest ab ye jaan hai 'Sauda'*
> *Phir aage dekhiye jo ho so ho, hua so hua*

THIS TOO WILL PASS

> Share not my fate with that heartless one, this too will
>   pass
> How the love-afflicted were undone, this too will pass

My tormentor, lest someone espy your stained
    garments
Wash off my blood from your red shirt-front, this too
    will pass

The wound has lanced my body; its pain has reached
    my heart
Call the surgeon to stitch it, someone! This too will
    pass

On hearing of my sorry fate, my heartless love said:
Don't harp on this tale, don't spoil the fun, this too
    will pass

Do not trouble your eyes on seeing my poor fortune
Why do those tears so copiously run? This too will
    pass

I sacrificed my love, my heart, my will—just life
    remains
Who can divine poor Sauda's fate? None, this too will
    pass.

KHWAJA MIR DARD

Another member of the 'Delhi school', Dard (1721–85) was a
Sufi, and also one of the first proponents of a very direct authorial
voice in the ghazal.[1] Mystical in bearing, he had a passion for
music, which is reflected in the rhythms of his poems. His ascetic
manner did not help him financially, as he refused all attempts
by local noblemen to patronize him in any way. In his own
eyes, Dard was truly a man of God. Representing the transitory
phase between Persian and Urdu, Dard wrote most of his prose
in Persian—a tome titled *Ilm-ul Kitaab* (The Knowledge of the
Book) is especially noteworthy—but began gravitating to the
people's tongue for his poetic output. His mysticism often cast
the world as a brief stop in a longer spiritual sojourn, and saw
death as just another move in that ongoing journey. In his most
famous sher, he conveys this with a simplicity that perhaps owes
a connection to Mir: '*Dosto dekha tamaasha yaan ke bas / Tum
raho ab ham to apne ghar chale*' ('Friends, I've had enough of
this display / I am off, if you wish, you can stay').

Interesting in this context is the defiant pose that Dard strikes
in the third couplet of this ghazal, vis-à-vis the religious straw
man (sheikh). The sher (which is one of Dard's most widely
quoted couplets and also famously performed by the singer
Mukesh) taunts the sheikh for viewing his soaked garments
(presumably with wine, since the maqta also extols drinking),
stating that if he were to wring his clothes, the angels would view

the squeezed liquid pure enough to use for their ablutions. The implicit celebration of the repudiation of religious strictures also characterizes Mir's work, and became an important element in the aesthetic traditions of the Delhi school.

HUM TUJH SE KIS HAVAS KI FALAK JUSTAJU KAREN

*Hum tujh se kis havas ki falak justaju karen
Dil hi nahin raha hai jo kuchh aarzoo karen*

*Mit jaayen ek aan mein kasrat numaiyaan
Hum aaine ke saamne aa kar jo 'hoo' karen*

*Har chand aainaa hoon par itnaa hoon na-qubool
Moonh pher le vo jis ke mujhe ru-ba-ru karen*

*Nai gul ko hai sabaat na ham ko hai aitbaar
Kis baat par chaman havas-e rang-o-bu karen*

*Hai apni ye salaah ke sab zahidaan-e shahr
Ai Dard aa ke bayat-e dast-e sabu karen*

SHOULD I ASK FATE FOR PASSION?

Should I ask fate for passion? I'm loath to do my part
I lost all desire when I lost my feckless heart.

All forms of consciousness will dissolve to one true
state
When I look at the mirror and proclaim God is great!

Sneer not, dear judgemental sheikh, at my clothes wet
    with wine
When they're wrung, angels ablute in this liquid
    divine.

I'm truthful like a mirror, but solitude's the price
Anyone who looks at me leaves, hates to remain near.

Spring I cannot guarantee, nor is the rose so strong
On whose hopes can gardens bloom, with colour,
    scent and song?

It's my advice, O Dard, to the city's puritans
That they shun their false gods, and to wine pay
    obeisance.

MIR TAQI MIR

In the pantheon of Urdu poetry, it is interesting to ask why it was only Mir (1723–1810) who came to be known as the *Khuda-e Sukhan* (God of Poetry). There is something originary about his work, which is not immediately apparent (just as a novice to cinema studies may not appreciate the trailblazing nature of *Citizen Kane* or *Battleship Potemkin* without an appreciation of the history of cinema itself). It is just that much of what is aesthetically brilliant about the ghazal seems to originate with Mir's work. The masters themselves, of course, paid obeisance. Consider for example this couplet by Ghalib: '*Rekhta ke tumhi ustad nahin ho Ghalib / Kehte hain agle zamane me koi Mir bhi tha*' ('You are not the only great exponent of Urdu, Ghalib / It is said that in the past there used to be a Mir as well').[1]

Mir's life coincided with a very eventful phase in India. On the one hand, he was accompanying his patrons to hunts (composing poems known as *shikar nama*s or hunt poems), writing his autobiography, revelling in his status as the poet laureate of the cognoscenti, and indulging his sensual desires.[2] On the other hand, his beloved Delhi was under such constant attack from serial marauders like Ahmed Shah Abdali that Mir had to move to Lucknow. His interactions with the Lucknow poets produced great strain because he had developed his own inflexible aesthetic and grew tired of their florid romanticism, while they found him puzzlingly quotidian (his clashes with the local star Sheikh Khalandar Bakht Jur'at remind one of the stand-offs between Shakespeare and Ben Jonson, with Mir standing in for Shakespeare).

In deference to Mir's exalted status, I have chosen to translate three of his poems here, all ghazals. The first one marked my personal entry point into his poetry, when I listened enthralled to Lata Mangeshkar's rendition of '*Dikhaai diye yoon ke bekhud kiya*' in the 1982 movie *Bazaar*. I would draw special attention to Mir's poignant maqta in this poem, which summarizes the essence of existential angst as depicted in romantic Urdu poetry.

The second ghazal, which I initially did not take to, mystified me because many Urdu poets themselves regard it as the finest ghazal ever written (Ghalib listed it among his favourites, especially the sher that went '*Naazuki us ke lab ki kya kahiye / Pankhudi ek gulaab ki si hai*').[3]

The final ghazal is also very celebrated, having been immortalized by the likes of singers such as Begum Akhtar, and also demonstrates Mir's sly asides at religion, which paved the way for a familiar anti-religious iconoclasm in Urdu literature. Mir's playful yet hard-hitting asides at religious orthodoxy (for example he says '*Dekhi hai jab se us but-e kaafir ki shakl, Mir / Jaata nahin hai jee tanik Islam ki taraf*'; 'Ever since I saw that infidel statue, Mir / My heart is not even mildly inclined toward Islam') set the tone for future poets to bring about an antagonistic and dialectical relationship between love and religion, a tradition that endures in Urdu poetry even today.

1 **FAQIRAANA AAYE**

> *Faqiraana aaye, sadaa kar chale*
> *Miyaan khush raho hum dua kar chale*

Jo tujh bin na jeene ko kahte the hum
So is ahd ko ab vafaa kar chale

Koi na-ummeedaana karte nigaah
So tum hum se moonh bhi chhupa kar chale

Bahut aarzoo thi gali ki teri
So yaan se lahu mein naha kar chale

Dikhaai diye yoon ke bekhud kiya
Hamein aap se bhi juda kar chale

Jabeen sajda karte hi karte gayi
Haq-e bandagi hum ada kar chale

Parastish ki yaan tak ke ai but tujhe
Nazar mein sabon ki Khuda kar chale

Kahen kya jo poochhe koi hum se Mir
Jahaan mein tum aaye the, kya kar chale?

I CAME LIKE A BEGGAR

Entering like a beggar, unfulfilled I went
Said a prayer for you mister, now be content

A promise I made not to stay alive without you
Now I leave the world to honour it, adieu

Any sign from you would confirm hopelessness
So you left sans a goodbye, hiding your face

To reach your street, was all that to me mattered
I arrived, but left defeated, blood-splattered

'Twas portrayed as a selfless quotidian act
But it tore me asunder from you in fact

My head prostrated before you on the ground
The essence of servitude, my love had found

So devout, O idol, was my faith in you
That in other eyes, I made you a God too

How should I respond, they ask me as I leave
In this stay on earth, Mir, what did you achieve?

2   HASTI APNI HUBAAB KI SI HAI

Hasti apni hubaab ki si hai
Ye numaaish saraab ki si hai

Naazuki us ke lab ki kya kahiye
Pankhudi ek gulaab ki si hai

Baar baar us ke dar pe jaata hoon
Haalat ab iztiraab ki si hai

Main jo bola kaha ke ye aawaaz
Usi khana-kharaab ki si hai

Mir, un neem-baaz aankhon mein
Saari masti sharaab ki si hai

MY LIFE, LIKE A BUBBLE, IS TRANSIENT

My life, like a bubble, is transient
This show, like a mirage, evanescent

Exquisite, those lips that lie in repose
Delicate as the petals of a rose

Again and again I go to that door
In a state of panic, need I say more?

I spoke and everyone guessed that this sound
Belonged perhaps to that wretched, cursed hound

Those half-lidded eyes of that love of mine
Mir, they bear all the headiness of wine.

3   ULTI HO GAEEN SAB TADBEEREIN

*Ulti ho gaeen sab tadbeerein, kuchh na dava ne kaam
      kiya*
Dekha? Is beemari-e dil ne aakhir kaam tamaam kiya

*Ahd-e jawani ro-ro kaati, peeri mein li aankhen
      moond*
Yaani raat bahut the jaage, subah hui, aaraam kiya

*Na-haq hum majbooron par ye tohmat hai mukhtari
      ki*
*Chaahte hain so aap kare hain, humko abas badnaam
      kiya*

Sarzad hum se be-adabi to wahshat mein bhi kum hi
hui
Koson us ki ore gaye par sajda har har gaam kiya

Mir ke deen-o-mazhab ko ab poochhte kya ho? Un
ne to
Qashqaa khencha, dair mein baithaa, kab ka tark
Islam kiya

ALL THOSE EFFORTS CAME TO NAUGHT

All those efforts came to naught, my wound no salve
could mend
See! This affliction of the heart beat me in the end.

I squandered youth in grief. Came age, I shut my
weary eye
I'd stayed awake all night—at dawn, I rested with a
sigh.

Prisoners of fate are termed players of the free-will game
How ironic, victims of caprice shoulder the blame.

I went mad but never broke devotion's protocol
Miles I walked toward you, bowed at each step, I
recall.

Ask not of Mir's faith, he's smeared ash-marks on his
forehead
He lives in temples, and from Islam's call, has long
fled.

NAZEER AKBARABADI

Widely credited with popularizing the nazm tradition in the ghazal-dominated canon of eighteenth-century Urdu poetry, Nazeer Akbarabadi, whose real name was Sheikh Wali Muhammad (1735–1830), chose to write in relatively accessible language. Like many who choose to experiment with simplicity, he paid a price when the elite saw his experiment as an aesthetic failure, i.e. an inability (rather than a refusal) to affect the florid rhythms that constituted the canon of his time. History, of course, has been kinder to Nazeer; he is now acknowledged as a true 'poet of the people' and his nazms hark back to a tradition where great poetry was sung in streets instead of being imprisoned unread in texts. The noted theatre artist Habib Tanvir based his famous play *Agra Bazaar* on Nazeer's life.

Nazeer's poetic reflection on mortality, *Banjaara Nama* (Gypsy Tale), has assumed the status of metaphor, with its refrain *'Sab thaath pada reh jaayega, jab laad chalega banjara'* ('All your pomp will stay behind when the gypsy loads up and walks off') now an acknowledged proverb in spoken Hindustani. He wrote plays on festivals like Diwali and Eid-ul Fitr, but chose to focus on their role as celebratory events rather than spiritual ones.

I have chosen to translate here a small part of his long poem titled *'Aadmi-Nama'* ('The Human Story'). Note that each verse has five lines; such a stanza is known as the mukhammas ('fiver'). The fifth lines form a refrain across verses (in this case, with

'. . . *hai so hai woh bhi hai aadmi*'). The simplicity of the verses likens the poem to a street ballad.

AADMI-NAMA

Duniya mein badshah hai so hai woh bhi aadmi
Aur muflis-o-gada hai so hai woh bhi aadmi
Zar-dar be-nawa hai so hai woh bhi aadmi
Ne'mat jo kha raha hai so hai woh bhi aadmi
Tukde jo mangta hai so hai woh bhi aadmi

Abdaal-o-qutb-o-ghaus-o-wali aadmi hue
Munkir bhi aadmi hue aur kufr se bhare
Kya kya karishme kashf-o-karamaat ke kiye
Hatta ke apne zor-o-riazat ke zor pe
Khaliq se ja mila hai so hai woh bhi aadmi

Fir'aun ne kiya tha jo daawa khudai ka
Shaddad bhi bahisht bana kar hua khuda
Namrud bhi khuda hi kahaataa thha bar mala
Yeh baat hai samajhne ki aage kahoon main kya
Yan tak jo ja chuka hai so hai woh bhi aadmi

Yaan aadmi hi naar hai aur aadmi hi noor
Yaan aadmi hi paas hai aur aadmi hi door
Kul aadmi ka husn-o-qaba mein hai yaan zahoor
Shaitaan bhi aadmi hai jo karta hai makr-o-zor
Aur haadi, rehnuma hai so hai woh bhi aadmi

Masjid bhi aadmi ne banaayi hai yaan miyaan
Bante hain aadmi hi imaam aur khutba-khwaan
Padhte hain aadmi hi namaaz aur quran yaan
Aur aadmi hi un ki churaate hain jootiyaan
Unko jo taad-ta hai so hai woh bhi aadmi

Yaan aadmi pe jaan ko ware hai aadmi
Aur aadmi hi tegh se maare hai aadmi
Pagdi bhi aadmi ki utaare hai aadmi
Chilla ke aadmi ko pukare hai aadmi
Aur sun ke daudhta hai so hai woh bhi aadmi!

THE HUMAN STORY

The king of this vast domain is also a man
And the beggar mendicant is also a man
The wealthy or the poorest is also a man
The one who eats sumptuously is also a man
And the one who begs for crumbs is also a man.

The sage, the saint, the prophet, yes—they all were
       men
The unbelievers, atheists, they too were men
The miracles they showed us were beyond our ken
They ruled us with the force of both the sword and
       pen
The creation who now seems a god? Also a man.

The Pharaoh did claim divinity, such were his lies
Shaddad made a city; called it his Paradise
Nimrod too decided to make the divine claim
What can I say? Fools! Their hubris was the same
The one who falls to such crass depths? Also a man.

Man is a blazing fire and the blessed light
It's man who's gone so far away, and is in our sight
It's man who is so beautiful and is so right
And man it is who represents Lucifer's blight
And he who saves us from perils? Also a man.

The mosques where we seek God's help—why are
    they man-made?
Men led the prayers and helped us pay spiritual dues
It was men who were lost in God, and while they
    prayed
Men they were too, who crept around and stole their
    shoes
The one who screams at those rascals? Also a man.

Who'll agree to sacrifice for another man?
Who'll smite a man with a sword? He too is a man.
Who will besmirch a man's reputation? A man!
Whom do the wretched call for redress? Yea, a man.
He who runs away, unheeding? Also a man.

INSHA

Insha Allah Khan 'Insha' (1756–1817) symbolized the ways in which one could claim, quite unselfconsciously, that Urdu and Hindi were truly the same language. The felicity with which he moved from his Persianized ghazals to his Hindi-identified poems like '*Rani Ketki ki Kahani*'[1] was not only wonderful but, as it were, unremarkable in those times. Unfortunately, he also epitomized the capricious future that lay in store for the poet who depended on royal patronage. Insha's best poems were written in his final days, as he, spurned by his sponsors and penniless, lost his beloved son to illness and death, and inhabited the twilight zone between grief and madness.

Of the two ghazals I translate here, the famous '*Insha-ji utho*' has been sung beautifully by Amanat Ali Khan, the maestro of the Patiala gharana. Mohammad Rafi sang his even more lugubrious and fatalistic '*Kamar baandhe hue*' as a non-film piece.

1   INSHA-JI UTHO

> *Insha-ji utho, ab kuchh karo, is shahr mein jee ka*
> *   lagaana kya?*
> *Vahshi ko sukoon se kya matlab? Jogi ka nagar mein*
> *   thikaana kya?*

Is dil ke dareeda-daaman ko dekho to sahi, socho to
 sahi
Jis jholi mein sau chhed hue us jholi ko phailaana
 kya?

Shab beeti chaand bhi doob gaya, zanjeer padi
 darvaaze mein
Kyon der gaye ghar aaye ho sajni se karoge bahana
 kya?

Us husn ke sanche moti ko hum dekh saken par
 chhoo na saken?
Jise dekh saken par chhoo na saken, vo daulat kya?
 Vo khazaana kya?

Jab shahr ke log na rasta den, kyon ban mein na ja
 bisraam kare?
Deevanon ki si na baat kare to aur kare deevana kya?

ARISE INSHA-JI

Arise, Insha-ji, let's depart
This city's no place to settle down
We are madmen, we abhor peace
Mendicants have no place in a town.

Cast a glance at your tattered soul
Ponder awhile, with reason calm
Your heart's but a shroud pierced with holes
Dare you use it to beg for alms?

The night is done, the moon is down
A strong secure chain locks your gate
How'll you explain to your love now
The reason you've returned this late?

Her beauty is a pearl, but I
Can merely watch but dare not touch
Such treasure is hardly worth much,
Eludes the grasp and haunts the eye.

If city-dwellers forsake me
Should I in forests seek respite?
I am fated to insane speech
For such talk is the madman's plight.

2   **KAMAR BAANDHE HUE**

*Kamar baandhe hue chalne ko yaan sab yaar baithe
        hain*
Bahut aage gaye, baaqi jo hain, taiyyar baithe hain

Na chhed ai nakhat-e baad-e bahaari raah lag apni
*Tujhe ath-kheliyaan soojhi hai, hum bezaar baithe
        hain*

Tasavvur arsh pe hai aur sar hai paa-e saaqi par
*Gharaz kuchh aur dhun mein is ghadi mai-khwaar
        baithe hain*

Bhalaa gardish falak ki chain deti hai kise, Insha?
*Ghaneemat hai ke ham-soorat yahaan do-chaar
        baithe hain*

READY TO LEAVE

My friends stand packed, ready to leave, determined,
    absolute
Some have left, the rest await departure, quite
    resolute

Bother me not, be on your way, O fragrant breeze of
    spring
I am at despair's door, while you wish to gambol and
    sing

Prostrate before the cupbearer, with thoughts that
    reach the sky
The drinkers sway to strange rhythms, while I silently
    sigh

Insha, seek no solace in this mad whirlpool of the
    fates
Be grateful that, in this strange land, you've found a
    few soulmates.

MIR ANEES

Mir Babar Ali Anees (1803–74) bestrode Urdu poetry like a colossus in the early nineteenth century, which is remarkable considering the fact that his poetry dealt nearly exclusively with religious themes and more specifically with the passion play of Karbala which dominates the religious narratives of Shia Islam. His contribution to the marsiya (or elegiac poetry) genre was so breathtaking that it informed the entire broader corpus of Urdu poetry. The marsiya is an epic poem with between 100 and 200 stanzas of six lines each, where, typically, the first four lines rhyme, as do the last two.[1]

For this volume, I have chosen to translate from two of Anees's poems, both regrettably brief. I began by translating a six-line verse from a marsiya that I placed in the introductory discussion on poetic form. The second piece that I have placed below comprises five verses of a marsiya, which is quite regularly performed at Shia religious gatherings called *majalis*. I have heard this poem since my childhood, and can never read or hear it without tears spontaneously welling up in my eyes. The verses I have chosen provide a unique tableau, where the unfolding drama of Imam Husain's sacrifice is being narrated to angels and prophets by God (indeed, to me it is metaphorically symmetrical that Anees has a God-like command over his language). God instructs his audience to see this moment of martyrdom as the ultimate expression

of closeness between the creator and the subject. The last verse
shifts the action back to the desert of Karbala, where Husain
is on the ground, and his executioner readies himself for the
final blow. In a few short verses Anees moves from grandeur
to pathos, from the depiction of Husain's power and stature
to that of his helplessness, from his exalted position in the
eyes of God to the utter hatred his killers exhibited toward
him and his family.

Readers may please note the similarities in language and
scene construction of Anees's and Dabeer's work to Brij Narain
Chakbast's verses about the Ramayana. The power of the
musaddas shines in the work of this triumvirate, even more
than in the hands of other exponents like Hali and Iqbal.

JAB PARESHAN HUI MAULA KI JAMAA'AT RAN MEIN

Jab pareshan hui maula ki jamaa'at ran mein
Har namaazi ko pasand aayi iqaamat ran mein
Qibla-e deen ne kiya qasd-e ibaadat ran mein
Shakl-e mehraab bani tegh-e shahaadat ran mein
Ghul hua, is ko Imam-e do-jahaan kehte hain
Teghon ke saaye mein Shabbir azaan kehte hain

Qudrat-e Haq se dareeche hue firdaus ke vaa
Daf-atan khul gaye dar-haa-e falak sar ta paa
Ek-ba ek uth gaye sab parda-e arsh-e aala
Ambiya-o-malak-o-hoor ko pahunchi ye sada
Qadr-daan is ka main hoon, mera shanaasa hai ye
Kyon na ho? Mere Mohammad ka navaasa hai ye.

Ye vo taa'at hai, ke tanhaa hi adaa karte hain
Mere aashiq tah-e shamsheer raha karte hain

> *Sar qalam hota hai, vo shukr-e khuda karte hain*
> *Sadiq-ul vaada yoonhi vaada vafaa karte hain*
> *Hum namaaz is ke janaaze ki jo padhwaaenge*
> *Tum bhi jaana ke rasoolan-e salaf jaayenge*
>
> *Saakin-e arsh-e bareen karne lage naala-o-aah*
> *Shah takbeer yahaan keh chuke, Allah Allah*
> *Aur iqaamat mein hue sarf shah-e alijaah*
> *Jaan-e vaahid pe gire aan ke laakhon badkhwaah*
> *Soora-e hamd nabizaada padha chaahta thha*
> *Shimr khanjar liye seene pe chada jaata thha*

WHEN FATE SCATTERED HUSAIN'S CONGREGATION IN THAT DESERT

When fate scattered Husain's congregation in that
    desert
The pious ones did praise his devotion on that desert
To pray, the Godhead showed his intention on that
    desert
A sword was raised, it sought execution on that
    desert.
A cry arose: indeed he is the leader of both worlds
Watch my brave Shabbir's call to prayer made in the
    shade of swords.

By his power, the Almighty bared heaven's great
    window
Suddenly the sky opened up its doors from head to toe
All curtains of the firmament opened to that scene's
    glow

Prophets and angels were summoned: 'Watch, and
    you need to know
That I am his admirer, to know me is in his blood
And why not? He's the grandson of my dear
    Mohammed.

'This is the sort of worship that is done only alone
Those who love me contend with swords, not with
    the kingly throne
They are beheaded and yet they prostrate to the One
They fulfil their promises, and then with this life are
    done.
When I convene the funeral prayer of this creation
    bold
You'd best attend, for you would join legions of
    prophets old.'

Heaven-dwellers began to weep at this great twist of
    fate
Husain composed himself to pray, proclaimed 'Allah
    is Great'
Alas till he finished his prayers, the killers refused to
    wait
Millions attacked that single soul, so vicious was their
    hate
As the Prophet's son read *soorah*s and repeated God's
    word
The murderous Shimr sat on him, lifting the fatal
    sword.

MIRZA DABEER

Mirza Salamat Ali Dabeer (1803–75), perhaps like the second man to walk the moon, was fated to coexist with a marginally more talented peer. Anees was considered the better *marsiyagoh*, which infuriated Dabeer, and which led to a lively rivalry between the two in Lucknow circles. Dabeer's verses tended to be more flowery, and he often experimented with form in the extreme, such as the time when he wrote an entire *benuqta* marsiya (one that did not use any word with a dot, equivalent in difficulty to someone writing a 700-line poem using only seventeen letters of the alphabet).

The marsiya tradition flourished in the expert hands of Dabeer because it allowed the poet to deal with a variety of emotions, using all manner of linguistic tropes and formulations. The snippet of marsiya I have translated below is structured as drama. The scene in my selected set of five verses involves the aftermath of the events of Karbala. Imam Husain's family, including his sister Bibi Zainab and his son Imam Ali bin Husain (both featured in the marsiya below) have been incarcerated in Damascus, and have been subjected to prolonged torture. At this moment, the wife of the tormentor Yazid (named Hind), who is a virtuous woman unaware of her husband's unspeakable tyranny, pays a visit to the prison. The first verse refers to Bibi Zainab's anguish and shame that she should be publicly visited at a moment of such vulnerability. The second and third speak of

Hind's consternation and grief at the desolation she encounters, while the fourth and fifth verses refer to her meeting with Imam Ali bin Husain, whom she sees as a young convict. Multiply the richness of these five verses by thirty, and one gets a sense of a single Dabeer marsiya. Now imagine hundreds of such marsiyas. These were some serious poets. For variety, I have chosen to translate Dabeer as free verse, rather than as my rhyme-bound translation of Anees.

QAIDKHAANE MEIN TALAATUM HAI KE HIND AATI HAI

Qaidkhaane mein talaatum hai ke Hind aati hai
Dukhtar-e Fatima ghairat se mui jaati hai
Rooh-e qaalib se vo zindaan mein ghabraati hai
Be-hawaasi se har ek baar vo chillati hai
'Aasman door zameen sakht kidhar jaaoon main?
Bibiyon mil ke dua maango ke mar jaaoon main.'

Naagahan Fizza ne di Ahl-e haram ko ye khabar
Hind aati hai bade jaah-o-tajammul se idhar
Bairqeen naqra-o-zar ki hai juloo ke andar
Sab kaneezen to rida odhe hain, vo nange sar
Par savaari bahut ahista ravaan hoti hai
Har qadam Hind thehar jaati hai aur roti hai

Kehti hai: 'Qaidiyon ke shor-o-bukaa ne maara
Mujh ko is "Hai Husaina" ki sadaa ne maara
In ke sardaar ko kya ahl-e jafaa ne maara?
Kya vo Sayyad thha jise ahl-e daghaa ne maara?
Ek bijli si kaleje pe mere girti hai
Nange-sar Fatima aankhon ke tale phirti hai!'

Laundiyaan thheen zan-e haakim ke jilaun mein jo ravaan
Dekhti kya hai ke ek sher hai aahan mein nihaan
Laaghar-o-khasta-tan-o-faaqa-kash-o-tashna-dahaan
Moonh pe seli ke nishaan, pusht pe durron ke nishaan
Saaq-e paa faaqe se zanjeer mein tharrati hai
Ustakhaanon se larazne ki sada aati hai.

Hind ne poochha 'Maraz kya hai?' Kaha 'Be-pidari'
Ro ke boli vo 'Dawaa kya hai?' Kaha 'Nauhagari'
Ghar jo daryaft kiya, kehne lage 'darbadari'
Boli leta hai khabar kaun? Kaha 'bekhabari
Kuchh kafan ke liye humraah nahin laaya hoon
Baap ko chhod ke be gor-o-kafan aaya hoon.'

THE PRISON IS IN TURMOIL, HIND'S ARRIVAL IS IMMINENT

The prison is in turmoil, Hind's arrival is imminent
The daughter of Fatima shrinks inwards in her shame
Her heart and soul are aflutter with fear in the
    dungeon
With unselfconscious passion, she lets out a scream
'The sky is too far, the earth too tough, where can I
    hide?
My sisters, pray that death should protect my dignity'

Suddenly Fizza announced to the Prophet's kin
'Hind arrives this way, with her dignified retinue
Her train is full of pomp and splendour,
But her head is bare though her companions are
    draped in shawls
The procession winds its way slowly, though
For at every step, Hind stops and begins to weep!'

Says she, 'The wails of these convicts will be the death
    of me
I have been slain by these shouts of "Alas, O Husain"
Who were the cruel ones who killed their leader?
Was he Mohammed's kin, the one murdered by
    tyrants?
A bolt of lightning strikes my heart
And in my eyes arises the image of Fatima,
    bareheaded!'

The women with the king's wife moved but she
    stopped
At the sight of a shackled youth, though tiger-like in
    bearing
Weak, emaciated, food-deprived, parched of tongue
With a face swollen by slaps, and a back scarred by
    the lash
His chains clattered with the tremble of his exhausted
    feet
His bones made sounds as if they creaked.

Asked Hind, 'What afflicts you?' He said,
    'Orphanhood.'
She wept. 'What is the cure?' 'Grief,' said he.
She asked for his address, and he said,
    'Homelessness.'
'And who cares for you?' He said, 'Anonymity.
Upon death, I have nothing that can serve me as a
    shroud
Indeed, I have left my father's corpse unclothed,
    unburied.'

BAHADUR SHAH ZAFAR

Few poets have had to practise their art in more trying circumstances than Zafar (1775–1862). He ascended the titular throne of the monarch of India in 1837, when the Mughal empire had shrunk to a size that was smaller than the current municipal limits of New Delhi. His desire to lead a life of leisure was to be rudely interrupted, however, when the first Indian war of independence was waged nominally under his flag by brave fighters who took on the world superpower of their time in 1857. The triumph of the British led to catastrophic consequences for Zafar, who was stripped of his emperorhood, watched his family members executed by the British forces, and eventually died in exile in Rangoon, leaving behind a *sardgah* (empty tomb) in Mehrauli, where he had wished to be interred next to his ancestors. His death ended the Mughal empire, and also marked the descent of Delhi into colonial servitude. In his words: '*Na ghar hai na dar hai, bacha ek Zafar hai, Faqat haal-e Dilli sunaane ki khaatir*' ('Without home or hearth we wander and we suffer, The sad tale of Delhi narrated by Zafar').

Much of Zafar's poetry was perhaps meant to presage his lonely fate.[1] His ghazals lend themselves to performance; and the three ghazals I have chosen to translate have been sung by a myriad of performers. My favourite renditions include Mehdi Hasan's essaying of '*Baat karni*'. Mohammad Rafi rendered '*Lagta nahin hai dil mera*' with his trademark simplicity

66

in the 1960 film *Laal Qila*. The fourth sher of this ghazal ('*umr-e daraaz...*'), about existential futility, has achieved metaphorical proportions in Urdu. Finally, his ghazal '*Shamsheer barahnaa*' was rendered by Preeti Sagar for Shyam Benegal's 1983 film *Mandi*. The sly verses compare the beauty of the beloved with the torment of the lover in interesting ways.

1   BAAT KARNI MUJHE MUSHKIL

> *Baat karni mujhe mushkil kabhi aisi to na thi*
> *Jaisi ab hai teri mehfil kabhi aisi to na thi*
>
> *Le gaya chheen ke kaun aaj tera sabr-o-qaraar*
> *Beqaraari tujhe ai dil kabhi aisi to na thi*
>
> *Un ki aankhon ne khuda jaane kiyaa kya jaadoo*
> *Ke tabiyyat meri maa'il kabhi aisi to na thi*
>
> *Chashm-e qaatil meri dushman thi hamesha lekin*
> *Jaise ab ho gayi qaatil kabhi aisi to na thi*
>
> *Aks-e rukhsaar ne kis ke hai tujhe chamkaayaa*
> *Taab tujh mein mah-e kaamil kabhi aisi to na thi*
>
> *Kya sabab tu jo bigadtaa hai Zafar se har baar*
> *Khoo teri hoor-e shamaa'il kabhi aisi to na thi*

I'M AT A LOSS FOR WORDS

I'm at a loss for words, it was never like this before
Your congregation now was never like this before.

Who is it then that has stolen my peace of mind
today?
Your consternation, O heart, was never like this
before.

God knows what magic it was that those eyes created
My heart's acute discomfort, was never like this before.

Your killer gaze, I always knew, would do me in some
day
The way it performed its task, was never like this
before.

Whose face is it that you reflect, tell me my dear full
moon?
Such beauty in your shine—it was never like this
before.

Why do you get so angry with Zafar time and again?
Your impatience, angel face, was never like this
before.

2   LAGTA NAHIN HAI JI MERA

Lagta nahin hai ji mera ujde dayaar mein
Kis ki bani hai aalam-e naa paayedaar mein

Bulbul ko paasbaan se, na sayyad se gila
Qismat mein qaid thhi likhi fasl-e bahaar mein

Keh do in hasraton se kahin aur jaa basein
Itni jagah kahaan hai dil-e daagdaar mein

Umr-e daraaz maang ke laaye thhe chaar din
Do arzoo mein kat gaye, do intezaar mein

Kitna hai bad-naseeb Zafar dafn ke liye
Do gaz zameen bhi na mili koo-e yaar mein

MY HEART IS UNEASY

In this deserted ruined space, uneasiness is great
To find some peace in this transient world was not my
fate.

The nightingale assigns no blame to the hunter, cage
or guard
Misfortune led it to spend youth in this captive state.

Tell my yearnings and desires that they may live
elsewhere
My heart alas is full of wounds, hardly the best estate.

Asked I for a wholesome life, but was granted four
mere days
For two I pined, and longed and yearned, and two I
spent in wait.

How unfortunate was Zafar that in death was denied
Two yards of earth for his grave in the lane of his
soulmate.

3   SHAMSHEER BARAHNAA

Shamsheer barahnaa maang ghazab, baalon ki mehak
phir vaisi hai

*Joode ki gundhaavat qahr-e khuda, zulfon ki latak
　　phir vaisi hai*

*Har baat mein us ke garmi hai, har naaz mein us ke
　　shokhi hai*
*Aamad hai qayaamat chaal bhari chalne ki phadak
　　phir vaisi hai*

*Mahram hai habaab-e aab-e ravaan sooraj ki kiran
　　hai us pe lipat*
*Jaali ki ye kurti hai vo balaa gote ki dhanak phir vaisi
　　hai*

*Vo gaaye to aafat laaye hai sur taal mein leve jaan
　　nikaal*
*Naach us ka uthaaye sau fitne ghunghroo ki chhanak
　　phir vaisi hai*

THE NAKED SWORD

Her hair's parting a naked sword, its fragrance is like
　　that
Its styling like the wrath of God, its fall is just like
　　that.

Her every word is packed with heat, her pride is
　　beauteous too
She enters like Armageddon, hips swaying just like
　　that.

The flowing rivers know her well, sunbeams confide
　　in her

Her shirt a diaphanous curse, her bangles clink just
  like that.

Her siren songs announce my doom, her rhythms take
  my life
Her dance causes a hundred fights, her anklets chime
  just like that.

ZAUQ

It was perhaps the misfortune of Zauq (1789–1854) that he happened to be the contemporary of the greatest poet in the Urdu pantheon, Ghalib. Like Antonio Salieri to Wolfgang Mozart in eighteenth-century Vienna, Zauq was to eclipse Ghalib in the Delhi mushaira circles of the mid-nineteenth century, and was even appointed poet laureate of the Mughal court while Ghalib languished in relative obscurity. But Zauq was smart enough to know genius when he encountered it; perhaps it was his own poetic ability that allowed him a glimpse into Ghalib's genius, and this aroused feelings of envy in him. The two are known to have had numerous verbal skirmishes. Of course, we now think of Ghalib, not Zauq, as the paradigmatic poet of nineteenth-century Delhi. But despite Ghalib's aura, Zauq's poetry continues to enthral. It is supposed that a large portion of his output was lost in the post-1857 chaos, but what is left includes a deevan[1]. Mohammad Husain Azad, the reported compiler of Zauq's surviving works, provides an extensive biography and critical comments on Zauq's work in his 1880 magnum opus *Aab-e Hayaat*[2].

The two ghazals translated here have been performed extensively by renowned singers.[3] The first verse of the second ghazal speaks of the existential angst that had permeated Urdu poetry in the nineteenth century, where the poets began to see themselves as mere puppets in a hostile tableau of history. This sentiment can be linked to some of Mir's more introspective works too, including some translated in this volume.

1 LAAYI HAYAAT AAYE

> *Laayi hayaat aaye, qazaa le chali, chale*
> *Apni khushi na aaye, na apni khushi chale*
>
> *Behtar to hai yahi ke na duniya se dil lagaye*
> *Par kya karen jo kaam na be-dillagi chale*
>
> *Ho umr-e Khizr bhi to kahenge ba waqt-e marg*
> *Ham kya rahe yahaan? Abhi aaye, abhi chale*
>
> *Duniya ne kis ka raah-e fanaa mein diya hai saath*
> *Tum bhi chale chalo yoon hi jab tak chali chale*
>
> *Naazaan na ho khirad pe jo hona hai vo hi ho*
> *Danish teri na kuchh meri daanishvari chale*
>
> *Kam honge is bisaat pe ham jaise bad-khumaar*
> *Jo chaal hum chale vo nihaayat buri chale*
>
> *Jaate havaa-e shauq mein hain is chaman se Zauq*
> *Apni balaa se baad-e saba ab kahin chale*

LIFE SUMMONED ME

> Life summoned me, I ascended; death caused my
>   descent
> Neither of my will I came, nor of my will I went.

It might be best not to fall for this world's wily snares
But some tasks just won't get done without love's
   droll consent.

Were we to be granted the age of Khizr[4], we would
   still
Say, 'Why leave now? I've just come! My passing, I
   resent!'

This world is indifferent to wayfarers bound for death
You may as well go on till your time here is spent.

Be not vain, knowledge will lose, fate has the upper
   hand
That which is decreed, none of your wisdom can
   prevent.

Few are worse than you once you've surrendered to
   the wine
What you did was truly mean, deserved is your
   torment.

Zauq flows away into the void from this verdant
   garden
After my death, should I care what spring and flowers
   had meant?

2   AB TO GHABRAA KE YE KAHTE HAIN

Ab to ghabraa ke ye kahte hain ke mar jaayenge
Mar ke bhi chain na paayaa to kidhar jaayenge?

Tum ne thahraai agar ghair ke ghar jaane ki
To iraade yahan kuchh aur thahar jaayenge

Hum nahin vo jo karen khoon ka daavaa tujh par
Balke poochhega khuda bhi, to mukar jaayenge

Aag dozakh ki bhi ho jaayegi pani pani
Jab ye aasi araq-e sharm se tar jaayenge

Shola-e aah ko bijli ki tarah chamkaaoon
Par mujhe dar hai, ke vo dekh ke dar jaayenge

Nahin paayegaa nishaan koi hamaara har-giz
Hum jahaan se ravish-e teer-e nazar jaayenge

Zauq, jo madarase ke bigde hue hain mullaah
Unko maikhaane mein le aao, sudhar jaayenge

IN FEAR YOU SAY

In fear you say you'd rather die, have you thought
    though?
If there is no solace in death, where will you go?

Since you wish to hedge bets, visit my rival's home
My fidelity will change too, it's quid pro quo.

I'll not blame you for my murder, even if God
Asks me. Immunity upon you, I'll bestow.

Hell's fire will lose its heat, turn into cold water
When we sinners pass wet in shame from head to toe.

I'll flash the flame of my pain like a lightning bolt
But will its light scare you away? I do not know.

You may search, but will never find a trace of me
I'll pass from sight like a glance, swift as an arrow.

O Zauq, for mullahs ruined by seminaries
A visit to yonder tavern may be apropos!

MIRZA GHALIB

Hoon garmi-e nishaat-e tasavvur se naghma-sanj
Main andaleeb-e gulshan-e na-aafareeda hoon

Behold, I sing in the heated joy of imagination
For I'm the nightingale of the yet uncreated garden.

The name of Mirza Asadullah Khan Ghalib (1797–1869) rolls
off the tongue like a word of gratitude. Indeed, Ghalib is a gift,
and he was well aware of it. In his own words, '*Surma-e muft-
nazar hoon, meri qeemat ye hai / Ke rahe chashm-e khareedaar
pe ehsan mera*' ('I am the kohl that adorns the eye, my only price
is your grateful sigh'). I am sighing.

What makes Ghalib so unique? Like Shakespeare in the
English dramatic tradition, he has now been studied so much
that all his poetic output has been subjected to the full glare of
scrutiny, and plumbed for metaphorical hints and allegorical
subtext. What made his poetry great was its simultaneous
accessibility and impenetrability. He could write the most playful
verses about mangoes and the most opaque verses about the
nature of existence. Consider the first sher of the first ghazal of
his deevan. It goes: '*Naqsh faryadi hai kis ki shokhi-e tehreer
ka / Kagazi hai pairahan, har paikar-e tasveer ka.*' The literal
translation of this two-liner could be: 'Whose creativity does the
creation complain about? / Every picture wears paper robes.'

77

This verse lends itself to multiple meanings, and is possibly the most analysed sher in the history of Urdu poetry.[1] Much has been said about the consternation of the poets in the Delhi mushaira circles—who were more used to lighter fare—when they heard such verses. The meaning of this famous verse actually hinges on a few metaphors. The wearing of paper robes refers to an ancient Persian custom in which complainants to the king dressed in paper to signify their unhappiness. Perhaps Ghalib is upset at God for the imperfection of his creation (the human); perhaps he is lauding humanity for its ability to critique God. In my opinion, a good translator would do well to not offer a direct interpretation of the sher, but rather alert the reader to the important elements of metaphor and context—and then promptly get out of the way.

We are also aware of a variety of anecdotes about his life that show him to be a colourful character. One anecdote has it that British soldiers once accosted him in a post-1857 round-up. The soldiers asked him, 'Are you a Muslim?' Ghalib replied, 'I am half-a-Muslim.' Watching their mystified expressions, he ventured a clarification: 'I drink liquor, but do not eat pork.' Likewise, his love for mangoes was well known. Once, his senior friend, a *hakim* (doctor), was watching Ghalib gorge on mangoes. He espied a donkey, which was rooting about in the garbage, but left a heap of mango peels alone. Hakim Saheb loftily remarked: 'Look Mirza, even the donkey does not like mangoes.' Never one to let such an opening go waste, Ghalib reparteed: 'True, Hakim Saheb, only a donkey would not like mangoes.'

Ghalib's witty anecdotes disparaging religion would fill pages, as would his sly asides at those in power, including those whom he depended on for financial assistance, and composed ceremonious odes to. His love life was chequered, his morals suspect, his sense of responsibility repugnant, but he was a character worthy of the appellation 'poet'.

Ghalib has been translated by several people, from language experts to armchair enthusiasts. It is refreshing to see him as the bone of contention among translators of varying temperaments, some of whom take extraordinary liberties with his work (for example, a recent book referred to his ghazals as 'sonnets'), while others take a more literal approach, choosing not to muck around with genius. I am an agnostic in this debate; I enjoy both kinds of efforts. Likewise, Ghalib has been the subject of relentless scholarly analysis. A friend who is an Urdu scholar estimates that over a thousand PhD theses have been done on Ghalib in India alone, and possibly as many in Pakistan. There are over twenty-five *sharah*s (explanatory volumes) of his deevan in print, many of which disagree quite violently on the meanings and contexts of his verse. I would recommend that the Ghalib neophyte start instead with a visual introduction—by watching Naseeruddin Shah portray him in Gulzar's magnificent TV serial.[2]

In deference to Ghalib's stature, I beg your indulgence for having chosen to translate five ghazals. I have translated only the first two rhythmically, choosing to let Ghalib's words speak for themselves in the other three without too much wordsmithing on my part. These ghazals have all been performed multiple times by a veritable pantheon of singers, and many performances are available in the public domain.[3]

1   AAH KO CHAAHIYE

> *Aah ko chaahiye ek umr asar hone tak*
> *Kaun jeeta hai teri zulf ke sar hone tak?*
>
> *Daam-e har mauj mein hai halqaa-e sadkaam-e*
>   *nahang*
> *Dekhen kya guzre hai qatre pe gohar hone tak*

Aashiqi sabr-talab aur tamanna betaab
Dil ka kya rang karoon khoon-e jigar hone tak

Hum ne maana ke taghaaful na karoge lekin
Khaak ho jaayenge hum tum ko khabar hone tak

Partav-e khur se hai shabnam ko fanaa ki taaleem
Main bhi hoon ek inaayat ki nazar hone tak

Ek nazar besh nahin fursat-e hasti ghaafil
Garmi-e bazm hai ek raqs-e sharar hone tak

Gham-e hasti ka, Asad, kis se ho juz marg ilaaj
Shama har rang mein jalti hai sahar hone tak

A CRY NEEDS

For a cry to lead to redress, it often takes an age
Who can remain alive while you with your stray curls
    engage?

Each wave of the ocean harbours a hundred crocodiles
What lies in store before the drop achieves a pearly
    stage[4]?

Love counsels patience while passion betrays its anxiety
How should I paint my bloodied heart while these
    duellists rage?

I know that you won't shrink from familiarity but
Before you hear of my sad plight, I would have died
    off-stage

The new sunbeam pronounces imminent death upon
     dewdrops
I too await the gaze that will both kill and assuage

A mere glance is sufficient for you to complete your
     task
A spark needs but a moment to kindle a fire's rage

What is the cure to life's sorrow save death, my dear
     Asad?
The taper burns all night, awaits the dawn to be
     upstaged.

2   BAS KE DUSHWAAR HAI

Bas ke dushwaar hai har kaam ka aasaan hona
Aadmi ko bhi mayassar nahin insan hona

Ishrat-e qatlgah-e ahl-e tamanna mat poochh
Eed-e nazaara hai shamsheer kaa uriyaan hona

Ki mere qatl ke baad us ne jafa se tauba
Hai us zood-pashemaan ka pashemaan hona

Haif us chaar-girah kapde ki qismat, Ghalib
Jis ki qismat mein ho aashiq ka garebaan hona

IT'S IMPOSSIBLE

It's impossible for all tasks to be facile, that's all
People find it so tough to answer humanity's call.

Measure not the desire for death in the passionate
The sight of the killer's sword presages the festival.[5]

After killing me, my tormentor forswore all murder
That swift repenter was contrite and rueful, I recall.[6]

Spare a thought for the ill-fated cloth of four
     measures that
Was destined to become a lover's shirt, tunic or shawl.[7]

3   SAB KAHAAN? KUCHH

Sab kahaan? Kuchh laala-o-gul mein numaayaan ho
     gai'n
Khaak mein kya sooratein hongi ki pinhaan ho gai'n

Yaad thi hum ko bhi ranga rang bazm-aaraaiyan
Lekin ab naqsh-o-nigaar-e taaq-e nisyaan ho gai'n

Thi banaatun-naash-e gardoon din ko parde mein nihaan
Shab ko un ke ji mein kya aaya ki uriyan ho gai'n

Joo-e khoon aankhon se bahne do ke hai shaam-e
     firaaq
Main ye samjhoonga ke shamen do farozaan ho gai'n

Neend uski hai, dimaagh uska hai, raatein uski hain
Teri zulfein jiske baazoo par pareshaan ho gai'n

Main chaman mein kya gaya, goya dabistan khul gaya
Bulbulen sun kar mere naale, ghazal-khwaan ho gai'n

Hum muvahhid hain, hamaara kaish hai tark-e
    rusoom
Millaten jab mit gai'n, ajzaa-e eemaan ho gai'n

Ranj se khoogar hua insaan to mit jaataa hai ranj
Mushkilen mujh par padi itni ke aasaan ho gai'n

Yoon hi gar rota raha Ghalib, to ae ahl-e jahaan
Dekhna in bastiyon ko tum, ke veeraan ho gai'n

NOT ALL, MERELY A FEW[8]

Not all, merely a few were celebrated in tulips and
    roses
What faces there must have been, which remain
    hidden in dust?

I remembered for a long time those colourful
    decorations
But now they are consigned to the shelf of forgotten
    memories.

The starry beauties of the constellation stayed hidden
    in the mist of the day
At night, wonder what came over them, they revealed
    themselves, disrobed[9].

Blood flows from my eyes; let it, for it's the night of
    separation
I will think of my burning eyes as two candles that
    were thus lit.

Sleep, and wisdom, and the nights all belong to that
   one
On whose shoulder you choose to rest, with your
   tresses scattered.

As I entered the garden, it was like school had
   commenced
The nightingales became poets, when they heard me
   declaim.[10]

I believe in Oneness, the disavowal of rituals is my
   creed
For when religions fade away, they will become part
   of true faith.

When one makes friends with grief, it miraculously
   disappears
I faced so many privations, that they eventually
   became facile.

If Ghalib keeps up his lament, mark my words O people
These neighbourhoods of yours will turn into
   wilderness.

4   HAZAARON KHWAAHISHEIN AISI

Hazaaron khwaahishein aisi ke har khwaahish pe
   dam nikle
Bahut nikle mere armaan, lekin phir bhi kam nikle

Nikalna khuld se Aadam ka sunte aaye hain lekin
Bahut be-aabroo ho kar tere kooche se ham nikle

Magar likhvaaye koi us ko khat to hum se likhvaaye
Hui subh aur ghar se kaan par rakh kar qalam nikle

Mohabbat mein nahin hai farq jeene aur marne ka
Usi ko dekh kar jeete hain jis kaafir pe dam nikle

Khuda ke vaaste parda na Kaabe se uthaa, zaalim
Kahin aisa na ho yaan bhi vahi kaafir sanam nikle

Kahaan maikhaane ka darvaza, Ghalib, aur kahaan
    vaaiz
Par itnaa jaante hain kal vo jaata thha, ke hum nikle

THOUSANDS OF DESIRES

Thousands of desires, and each one worth dying for
Many of my desires were fulfilled, but yet, I feel
    unrequited.

We have heard often of the expulsion of Adam from
    Eden
But that is nothing compared to my shamed exit from
    your street.

If anyone wishes to write my love a letter, then I am
    available
Every morning, I set out, with a pen tucked behind
    my ear.[11]

In love, there is no difference between living and dying
For I find my will to live by gazing at the infidel who
    kills me.[12]

For God's sake, keep the black cloth on the Kaaba
I do not want to find that it harbours yet another
    infidel idol.[13]

Whither the tavern door, Ghalib, and whither the
    holy man?
But I swear, as I left the winehouse last night, I saw
    him enter.

5   **BAAZEECHA-E ATFAAL**

Baazeecha-e atfaal hai duniya mere aage
Hota hai shab-o-roz tamaasha mere aage

Hota hai nihan gard mein sehraa mere hote
Ghista hai jabeen khaak pe dariya mere aage

Mat poochh ke kya haal hai mera tere peechhe
Tu dekh ke kya rang hai tera mere aage

Eemaan mujhe roke hai jo khenche hai mujhe kufr
Kaabaa mere peechhe hai, kaleesa mere aage

Go haath ko jumbish nahin aankhon mein to dam hai
Rehne do abhi saaghar-o-meenaa mere aage

Hum-pesha-o-hum-masharab-o-humraaz hai meraa
Ghalib ko buraa kyon kaho achhaa mere aage

THE PLAY OF CHILDREN

The world to me is no more than a play of children
This cheap spectacle occurs every day in front of me.

[For the dust my wandering raises] the desert
    acknowledges my superiority
[For the volume of my tears] the sea acknowledges me
    as its master.[14]

Ask not how I am doing in your absence
Instead, watch your colour in my presence.[15]

Faith compels me to stop, while infidelity pulls me
    forward
I vacillate thus, between the Kaaba and the church.

Admittedly, my hands have ceased to move, but my
    eyes still have strength
Keep the cask and the wine glass in front of me.[16]

He shares my profession, my wine, and also my
    secrets
And you dare denounce 'Ghalib' in front of me!

MOMIN

It is reported that when Ghalib heard Momin Khan Momin's (1800–51) sher that went '*Tum mere paas hote ho goya / Jab koi doosra nahi hota*' ('It is as if you are close to me / When there is nobody else'), he offered an extraordinary trade: his entire deevan for that one couplet. I hope Ghalib was not serious, but if he was, I'd recommend Momin run, not walk, to accept the trade! Nevertheless, it is good to be appreciated thus by the master. Many of Momin's verses have been elevated to the status of metaphor in standard Urdu usage. For example, on the persisitence of habit: '*Umr saari to kati ishq-e butaan mein, Momin, / Aakhri waqt mein kya khaak musalmaan honge*' ('I have spent my life loving idols, Momin, / On my deathbed, I am loath to accept Islam').

A hakim by profession, Momin also dabbled in mathematics, was a musician, and was known to have played a mean game of chess. His epicurean life unfortunately ended in an ultra-religious phase, which must have made some of his naughtier verses very sad.

I include here what is perhaps the best-known ghazal by Momin: '*Vo jo hum mein tum mein qaraar thha*'.[1]

VO JO HUM MEIN TUM MEIN QARAAR THHA

Vo jo hum mein tum mein qaraar thha, tumhe yaad
ho ke na yaad ho

88

Vahi yaani vaada nibaah ka tumhe yaad ho ke na
*   yaad ho*

Vo naye gile vo shikaayaten, vo maze maze ki
*   hikaayaten*
Vo har ek baat pe roothna tumhe yaad ho ke na yaad
*   ho*

Koi baat aisi agar hui jo tumhaare ji ko buri lagi
To bayan se pahle hi bhoolna tumhe yaad ho ke na
*   yaad ho*

Suno zikr hai kai saal kaa, koi vaadaa mujh se tha
*   aap ka*
Vo nibaahne kaa to zikr kya, tumhe yaad ho ke na
*   yaad ho*

Kabhi hum mein tum mein bhi chaah thi, kabhi hum
*   se tum se bhi raah thi*
Kabhi hum bhi tum bhi thhe aashna, tumhe yaad ho
*   ke na yaad ho*

Vo bigadnaa vasl ki raat kaa, vo na maan-na kisi baat
*   ka*
Vo nahin nahin ki har-aan adaa, tumhe yaad ho ki na
*   yaad ho*

Jise aap ginte thhe aashnaa, jise aap kehte thhe
*   baavafaa*
Main vahi hoon Momin-e mubtalaa tumhe yaad ho ke
*   na yaad ho*

THAT FAMILIARITY BETWEEN US

That familiarity between us
You may remember perhaps, perhaps not
Those days we made each other promises
You may remember perhaps, perhaps not.

Your annoyed reproach at matters minor
They led me to label you a whiner
At every moment, your feigned distress
You may remember perhaps, perhaps not.

Perchance if something had really hurt you
You would forget in an instant, I knew
Your wonderful forgiving affections thus
You may remember perhaps, perhaps not.

I recall a promise you made years ago
It remains unfulfilled, don't you know?
Is this matter unfit for us to discuss?
You may remember perhaps, perhaps not.

Your anger at me on our union right
When you perceived my actions as a slight
The words 'no, no' the way I saw you stress
You may remember perhaps, perhaps not.

The one you found trustworthy to the end
The one you always counted a friend
I remain that Momin, I do profess
You may remember perhaps, perhaps not.

DAGH DEHLAVI

Nawab Mirza Khan is hardly a household name among Urdu enthusiasts, but the *Urdu-daan*s of Delhi and Hyderabad bare their fangs when they dispute the affiliations of Dagh (1831–1905), who lived much of his life in Delhi but chose to move south after the 1857 upheaval and its aftermath. Dagh wrote many of his famous ghazals after he moved southward[1], and his grave near the Yusufain Dargah is still a site of pilgrimage to Hyderabadis. He is most notably invoked by oldies when they quote the first line of the following sher as they sit down: '*Hazrat-e Dagh jahaan baith gaye, baith gaye / Aur honge teri mehfil se nikalne vale*' ('Where Sir Dagh sits, he stays seated / There may be others who choose to exit your presence').

The two ghazals I have chosen to translate are among his more popular ones.[2]

1   JI JAANTA HAI

> *Lutf vo ishq mein paaye hain ke ji jaanta hai*
> *Ranj bhi, taane uthaaye hain ke ji jaanta hai*

> *Jo zamaane ke sitam hain vo zamaana jaane*
> *Tu ne dil itne dukhaaye hain ke ji jaanta hai*

Tum nahin jaante ab tak ye tumhaare andaz
Vo mere dil mein samaaye hain ke ji jaanta hai

Inhin qadmon ne tumhaare, inhin qadamon ki qasam
Khaak mein itne milaaye hain ke ji jaanta hai

Dosti mein teri dar-parda hamaare dushman
Is qadar apne paraaye hain ke ji jaanta hai

ONLY THE HEART KNOWS

Such pleasure in love I have found, only the heart
    knows
Sometimes taunts, sometimes grief profound, only the
    heart knows.

Let us leave time alone to deal with its tyrannies
Of the souls that you have drowned, only the heart
    knows.

You do not know this yet but your careless flirtations
In my earnest mind, abound; only the heart knows.

Your feckless feet, I swear on your cavalier feet
Many they have into dust ground, only the heart
    knows.

The distinction between friend and foe is no longer
    clear
Such taxonomies do confound, only the heart knows.

2   SABAQ AISA

Sabaq aisa padha diya tune
Dil se sab kuchh bhula diya tu ne

Hum nikamme hue zamaane mein
Kaam aisa sikha diya tu ne

Laakh dene ka ek dena hai
Dil-e be-mudda diya tu ne

Be-talab jo mila mila mujhko
Be gharaz jo diya diya tu ne

Kahin mushtaq se hijab hua
Kahin parda utha diya tu ne

Mit gaye dil se naqsh-e baatil sab
Naqsha apna jama diya tu ne

Dagh ko kaun dene waala thha?
Jo diya, ai khuda diya tu ne.

SUCH A LESSON

Indeed, such a lesson you have taught
All previous knowledge my heart forgot.

I've been rendered useless to the world
Such fruits your feckless labours have wrought.

Priceless is the gift that you gave me
A content heart that no longer sought.

I received without seeking bounties
You gave me with future motives, naught.

Sometimes you gave, veiled and secretly
Sometimes you were obvious, a lot.

Your visage became so clear, that I
Forgot that your face was with evil fraught

Who else will give with such great elan?
Who else but God, that's what 'Dagh' thought.

MAULANA HALI

When he was a young poet, Maulana Altaf Husain Hali (1837–1914) recited his work in front of Ghalib, who is said to have approved. But 1857 intervened, and he returned from Delhi to Panipat. Eventually, he made the acquaintance of Sayyid Ahmad Khan and, at his behest, went about composing an epic poem *Musaddas-e Madd-o Jazr-e Islam* (A Musaddas on the Ebb and Flow of Islam). The poem was published in 1879, and is now known simply as *Musaddas-e Hali*. It critiques the Muslims of Hali's era as decadent when compared to the glory of Islamic history; however, despite this self-reflexivity, it is not difficult to see how such narratives presented a defensive posture, given the ascendency of the West and the 'victory' of the colonists (Ashis Nandy reflects about similar tendencies in Swami Vivekananda's thought in his book *The Intimate Enemy*). Depending on one's perspective, it is ironic or fitting to see these ideas being expressed by a poet with the takhallus 'Hali' (meaning 'of the present'). One may mention in passing that Hali wrote perhaps the first biography of Ghalib, titled *Yaadgaar-e Ghalib*. His *Muqaddama-e Sher-o-Shairi* (Exegesis on Poems and Poetry) remains one of the earliest works of literary criticism in Urdu.

In this collection, I am translating one of his more famous ghazals.

HAI JUSTAJU

Hai justaju ke khoob se hai khoobtar kahaan
Ab dekhiye thaharti hai jaa kar nazar kahaan

Yaarab is ikhtilaat ka anjaam ho ba-khair
Tha us ko hum se rabt, magar is qadar kahaan

Ek umr chaahiye ke gawaaraa ho naish-e ishq
Rakhhi hai aaj lazzat-e zakhm-e jigar kahaan

Hum jis pe mar rahe hain vo hai baat hi kuchh aur
Aalam mein tujh se laakh sahi, tu magar kahaan

Hoti nahin qubool dua tark-e ishq ki
Dil chaahta na ho to zuban mein asar kahaan

Hali, nishaat-e naghma-o-mai dhoondte ho ab
Aaye ho waqt-e subh, rahe raat bhar kahaan

MY AMBITION

To be better than the best, that is my ambition
Let us see where my sight rests, ends its exploration

O God, I pray this intimacy ends happily
Love was warm before, but this is fiery ignition

Verily, it takes an age to get used to love's pain
The wounded heart slowly makes friends with its
    condition

Thus far I had been taken in by a strange visage
I want you, not someone like you, an apparition

My prayer that love should vanish remains
    unanswered
For the heart does not back up the tongue's
    composition

Hali arrives in the morn seeking wine and song
Whose company caused you to miss the night's
    edition?

AKBAR ALLAHABADI

Syed Akbar Husain, aka Akbar Allahabadi (1846–1921), was a great satirist who unfortunately sobered down and became serious, mystical and religious (in other words, boring) in his later days. I enjoy his earlier poems; they are elaborate jokes set to verse. His later poetry exhibits a more classical mindset, which, while competent, is not as delightful. He was part of a lively debate among the Urduwalas of the late nineteenth century, and opposed his peers like Sir Sayyid for their allegiance to Western mores. Even his conservatism was imbued with wit; opposing the practice of women renouncing the veil, he composed the following qataa:

> *Be-parda kal jo aayi nazar chand beebiyaan*
> *Akbar zameen mein ghairat-e qaumi se gadh gaya*
> *Poochha jo main ne aap ka parda, vo kya hua?*
> *Kehne lageen ke aql pe mardon ke padh gaya.*

> Yesterday, as some bareheaded ladies walked down
>   the lane
> Akbar bemoaned his culture with a sense of shame
>   and pain
> I asked politely, 'Ladies, how come you have lost your veil?'
> Said they, 'That opaque cloth resides now on our
>   menfolk's brain.'

I have translated two poems below. The first is a classical ghazal that was sung by the maestro K.L. Saigal, while the second is a comic poem about an imaginary dialogue between Majnu and Laila's mother. The social criticism of indolent Indians, especially Muslims, is difficult to miss. Muslim culture of a certain social class tended to devalue labour and trade, and Akbar provides an ironic critique of this. I have translated the second verse in jaunty language to preserve its affect.

1   DUNIYA MEIN HOON

> *Duniya mein hoon duniya ka talabgaar nahin hoon*
> *Bazaar se guzra hoon, kharidaar nahin hoon*
>
> *Zindaa hoon magar zeest ki lazzat nahin baaqi*
> *Har-chand ke hoon hosh mein, hoshiyaar nahin hoon*
>
> *Is khaanaa-e hasti se guzar jaaoonga be-laus*
> *Saayaa hoon faqat naqsh-ba deevaar nahin hoon*
>
> *Afsurda hoon ibrat se dava ki nahin haajat*
> *Gham ka mujhe ye zof hai beemar nahin hoon*
>
> *Vo gul hoon khizaan ne jise barbaad kiya hai*
> *Uljhoon kisi daaman se main vo khaar nahin hoon*
>
> *Yaarab mujhe mahfooz rakh us but ke sitam se*
> *Main us ki inaayat ka talab-gaar nahin hoon*
>
> *Afsurdagi-o-zauf ki kuchh had nahin, Akbar*
> *Kaafir ke muqaabil mein bhi deen-daar nahin hoon*

I'M IN THIS WORLD

I'm in this world but I'm not consumed by its desire
I did pass by the market, but I am no customer

I am alive, but life to me is bereft of pleasure
I am smart but don't call me devious. That is a slur

From this house that represents life I will exit
    unspoiled
I am no imprint on the wall, but a shadow, a blur

My conscience is enough for me, I need no sage advice
I'm sick with grief but I'm not ill, no potions for me, sir

I am the flower that has been done in by autumn's
    blight
To be the thorn that rends clothes, such a life I don't
    prefer

O God, keep me safe from the tyranny of that idol
I am not desirous of the largesse that it might confer

My sadness and self-abasement have no limits,
    Akbar
I've less faith than the infidel, with this you must
    concur

2 LAILA KI MAA AUR MAJNU

Khudahafiz musalmanon ka Akbar
Mujhe to un ki khush-haali se hai yaas

Yeh ashiq shahid-e maqsood ki hein
Na jaayenge, wa lekin sayi ke paas

Sunaoon tum ko ek farzi lateefa
Kiya hai jis ko main ne zeb-e qirtaas

Kaha Majnu se ye Laila ki maa ne
Ke 'Beta, tu agar kar le MA pass

'To fauran byaah doon Laila ko tujh se
Bila diqqat main ban jaaoon teri saas'

Kaha Majnun ne 'Ye achhi sunaai!
Kuja aashiq, kuja college ki bakvaas

'Badi bee, aap ko kya ho gaya hai
Hiran pe laadi jaati hai kahin ghaas?

'Ye achhi qadr-daani aap ne ki
Mujhe samjha hai koi Harcharan Das?

'Yehi thhehri jo shart-e vasl-e Laila
To istefa mera ba hasrat-o-yaas.'

LAILA'S MOTHER AND MAJNU

May Allah keep all Muslims in his shelter, O Akbar
I pray for their happiness and their well-being as a rule

They love their Prophet who bore witness to his Creator
They will go to their happy fate, and drink from
heaven's pool

I will share with you an imagined tale for your
    pleasure
That I have composed, I'm sure you'll find it cool

Said Laila's mother to Majnu, the suffering paramour
'Dear son, all you have to do is to go to graduate
    school

'Then I will immediately accept you as my son-in-law
And be your mom-in-law and stop treating you like a
    ghoul'

Majnu started: 'Hey wait a sec, I don't think I heard
    right
A Romeo and higher studies? Don't take me for a fool

'You've got it all wrong, old lady, why don't you
    watch your mouth
A deer is no beast of burden, don't load me like a
    mule

'This is a strange way to treat guests, have you no
    manners, ma'am?
I am no Harcharan Das, your proposal's rather cruel

'If this is the condition of union with your daughter
Please accept my resignation, I'm sad, but I'm no
    tool.'

MOHAMMED IQBAL

What can I say about Allama Iqbal (1877–1938) that has not been repeated a million times before? A beautiful website devoted to him is maintained by the Iqbal Academy Pakistan[1], and he has his own YouTube channel as well. V.G. Kiernan's 1955 book of translations of his poetry has been reissued.[2] A listing of books devoted to him would be far too immense a task to do justice to; indeed, a few bibliographies of books on Iqbal have been published as books in their own right.

But to scratch that formidable surface that is the persona of the 'Poet of the East', let us say that he had a doctorate in philosophy from the University of Heidelberg, that he wrote the most amazing poems in a language that was not his mother tongue, and that when he died in 1938, his funeral was attended by 70,000 people, which included colonialists and freedom fighters, the atheists of the PWA and the fundamentalists of the *Ahl-e Hadees*, Indian nationalists and Muslim Leaguers, reflecting his ability to defy categorization. I personally find Iqbal to be much more of a progressive; his engagement with Islam is critical and borderline heretical. His protagonist asserts selfhood against God in *Shikva*, his long musaddas, often mocking the creator. One of my brother's favourite poems is Iqbal's '*Gibreel aur Iblees*' (Gabriel and Satan) where Lucifer (Iblees) mocks Gabriel for his blind faith, while proudly asserting that it is his disobedience to God that has imbued the story of creation with life.[3]

Here, I have translated two poems, the first as free verse and the second more rhythmically. The first is a ghazal, which was sung beautifully by Nusrat Fateh Ali Khan. The second, titled '*Farmaan-e Khuda Farishton se*' (God's Command to the Angels), is from Iqbal's book *Baal-e Gibreel* (Gabriel's Wing), and is a response by God to Lenin. The previous poem in that collection is called '*Lenin, Khuda ke Huzoor Mein*' (Lenin in God's Presence), where Lenin has complained to God about injustice. Such an imaginary dialogue is vintage Iqbal, in the vein of the aforementioned *Shikva* and '*Gibreel aur Iblees*'. Lenin holds his ground, accusing God of being ineffectual, while God is not upset at all with Lenin's impertinence. Instead, in response to the diatribe, He calls upon His angels to effect a few changes in the organization of the world at large. Wouldn't you have liked to be a fly on the wall during that exchange? Thanks to Iqbal, you were.

1   KABHI AI HAQEEQAT-E MUNTAZAR

> *Kabhi ai haqeeqat-e muntazar, nazar aa libaas-e*
> *majaz mein*
> *Ke hazaaron sajde tadap rahe hain meri jabeen-e*
> *niyaaz mein*
>
> *Tu bachaa bachaa ke na rakh ise, teraa aaina hai vo aaina*
> *Ke shikasta ho to azeez-tar, hai nigaah-e aaina-saaz mein*
>
> *Na kaheen jahaan mein amaan mili, jo amaan mili to*
> *kahaan mili*
> *Mere jurm-e khaanaa kharaab ko, tere afv-e banda-*
> *navaaz mein*

*Na vo ishq mein rahi garmiyaan, na vo husn mein
    rahin shokhiyaan*
*Na vo Ghazanavi mein tadap rahi, na vo kham hai
    zulf-e Ayaaz mein*

Jo main sar-ba-sajda hua kabhi to zameen se aane lagi sadaa
*Tera dil to hai sanam-aashna, tujhe kya milega
    namaaz mein*

FOR ONCE, O LONG-SOUGHT TRUTH

For once, O long-sought truth, appear before me, in
    understood metaphor
For a thousand obeisances wait in my forehead,
    awaiting consummation

Do not keep your heart so safe, for it is such a mirror
That it increases in value only after it has been
    shattered

I found no solace in this world, except now, when
My unforgivable sin was housed by your infinite
    forgiveness

Neither does love have that heat any more, nor
    beauty the allure
Neither has Ghazni that passion, nor Ayaz the beauty[4]

When I prostrated my head, a voice arose from the earth
Your heart loves but an idol, what will you find in
    Allah's prayer?

2   **FARMAN-E KHUDA (FARISHTON SE)**

Uthho meri duniya ke ghareebon ko jagaa do
Kaakh-e umaraa ke dar-o-deevaar hila do

Garmaao ghulaamon ka lahu soz-e yaqin se
Kunjishk-e phiromaayaa ko shaaheen se lada do

Sultaani-e jamhoor ka aata hai zamaana
Jo naqsh-e kuhan tum ko nazar aaye mita do

Jis khet se dah-qaan ko mayassar nahin rozi
Us khet ke har khosha-e gandum ko jala do

Kyon khaaliq-o-makhlooq mein haayal rahen parde
Peeraan-e kaleesa ko kaleesa se hata do

Main naakhush-o-bezaar hoon marmar ke silon se
Mere liye mitti kaa haram aur bana do

Tahzeeb-e naveen kaar-gah-e sheesha-garaan hai
Aadab-e junoon shaayar-e mashriq ko sikha do

GOD'S BIDDING TO THE ANGELS

Go bid the wretched of my earth to awake
The foundations of elite palaces should quake

Roil the blood of slaves with the pain of belief
Sparrows should challenge eagles, make no mistake

The moment of democracy is at hand
Signs of the old order I bid thee to break

Burn every ear of wheat of that field from which
The farmer is not permitted to partake

Distance between God and humans is futile
Remove the bishops from the church; they are fake

Build me a simple house with sand, for I hate
Those marble edifices. That's a mistake.

The new world is but a brittle glass palace
Poet of the East, learn madness and heartache.

BRIJ NARAIN CHAKBAST

Chakbast (1882–1926) was one of the foremost lawyers of Lucknow in the early twentieth century. A veteran of the freedom movement, he wrote eloquently in support of 'home rule', as independence was termed in those days. His first book, titled *Subh-e Watan* (Morning in the Homeland), was published in 1931, five years after his death. He wrote in a variety of formats, including the ghazal. The sher from his collection that became most famous was:

> *Zindagi kya hai anasir mein zahur-e tarteeb*
> *Maut kya hai inhi ajza ka pareshan hona*

> Life,
> When elements become ordered, that's all
> Death,
> But a moment when into chaos they fall

Chakbast would, however, achieve immortality for his Ramayan poems. He wrote three, each a masterpiece in the musaddas tradition. They were 'Ramayan ka Ek Scene' ('A Scene from the Ramayana'), 'Maa ka Javaab' ('The Mother's Response'), and 'Vanvaas par Ayodhya Nagri ki Haalat' ('The State of Ayodhya during the Exile').[1] I have translated an excerpt from 'Ramayan ka Ek Scene' that depicts the moment Lord Rama,

108

who has been banished from Ayodhya for fourteen years, takes his final leave of his mother Kausalya.

RAMAYAN KA EK SCENE[2]

Rukhsat hua vo baap se le kar khuda ka naam
Raah-e vafaa ki manzil-e awwal hui tamaam
Manzoor tha jo maa ki ziyaarat ka intezaam
Daaman se ashk pochh ke dil se kiya kalaam
Izhaar-e bekasi se sitam hoga aur bhi
Dekha hamen udaas to gham hoga aur bhi

Dil ko sambhaalta hua aakhir vo nau-nehaal
Khaamosh maa ke paas gaya surat-e khayaal
Dekha to ek dar mein hai baithi vo khasta haal
Sakta sa ho gaya hai, ye hai shiddat-e malaal
Tan mein lahoo ka naam nahin, zard rang hai
Goya bashar nahin, koi tasveer-e sang hai

Kya jaane kis khayaal mein gum thi vo begunaah
Noor-e nazar pe deeda-e hasrat se ki nigaah
Jumbish hui labon ko, bhari ek sard aah
Li gosha haai chashm se ashkon ne rukh ki raah
Chehre ka rang haalat-e dil kholne laga
Har moo-e tan zaban ki tarah bolne laga

Ro kar kaha; khamosh khade kyon ho meri jaan?
Main jaanti hoon, kis liye aaye ho tum yahaan
Sab ki khushi yahi hai tu sahra ko ho rawaan
Lekin main apne moonh se na hargiz kahoongi 'haan'
Kis tarah ban mein aankh ke taare ko bhej doon?
Jogi bana ke raaj dulaare ko bhej doon?

Duniya ka ho gaya hai ye kaisa lahoo safed?
Andha kiye hue hai zar-o-maal ki ummed
Anjaam kya hai? Koi nahin jaanta ye bhed
Soche bashar, to jism ho larzaan misaal-e baid
Likkhi hai kya hayaat-e abad in ke waaste?
Phaila rahe hain jaal ye kis din ke waaste?

Leti kisi faqeer ke ghar mein agar janam
Hota na meri jaan ko samaan ye baham
Dasta na saanp ban ke mujhe shaukat-o-hasham
Tum mere laal, thhe mujhe kis saltanat se kam?
Main khush hoon, phoonk de koi is takht-o-taaj ko
Tum hi nahin, to aag lagaaoongi raaj ko

Sun kar zaban se maa ki ye faryaad dard khez
Us khasta jaan ke dil pe chali gham ki tegh-e tez
Aalam ye tha qareeb, ke aankhen hon ashk rez
Lekin hazaar zabt se rone se ki gurez
Socha yehi, ke jaan se bekas guzar na jaaye
Nashaad hum ko dekh ke maa aur mar na jaaye

Phir arz ki ye maadar-e nashaad ke huzoor
Mayoos kyon hain aap? Alam ka hai kyon wufoor?
Sadma ye shaaq aalam-e peeri mein hai zaroor
Lekin na dil se keejiye sabr-o-qaraar door
Shayad khizaan se shakl ayaan ho bahaar ki
Kuchh maslahat isi mein ho parwardigaar ki

A SCENE FROM THE RAMAYANA

He said goodbye to his father taking the name of God
The first step on fidelity's tough path his feet had trod

Now for a meeting with his mother he began to plod
Wiping his tears he spoke inward squaring his
    shoulders broad
'I dare not let her see my pain; it will cause her more
    grief
Better I show a smiling face that may give her relief.'

Thus steeling his sad heart, the youth began to move
    at last
He reached but found her silent, lost in her own
    thoughts, downcast
Alone in a doorway, though contemplating something
    vast
He'd braced for tears but was rendered dumbstruck
    by this contrast
Her body appeared bloodless, her colour yellow and
    pale
As if she was no human form but a stone statue, frail

Wonder what passed through the mind of that woman
    innocent
She cast a glance at her scion, her gaze like a lament
Her lips quivered as if she would give voice to her
    torment
Finally grief moved from her heart and to her eyes it went
The colour of her face began to portray her heart's plight
Her grief became a tongue itself, and commenced to
    recite

With weeping eyes she asked her son, 'Why don't you
    speak your mind?
I know what errand brings you here, what puts you in
    a bind

"Everyone will be happy if I leave," you have divined
But I will never permit you to go, let me remind
You that you are my shining star, I'll never let you go
Like a yogi to the forest, I must say no, no, no.

'Has this world lost its loyalty, why has our blood
    turned white?
Has the desire for wealth and fame caused us to lose
    our sight?
How will this sorry story end? It will only cause
    blight
I quiver like a reed when I imagine my son's plight
My question is to those people who are planning this
    strife
Do they plan to live forever? Don't they fear the
    afterlife?

'Had I been born a beggar's girl, this would not be my
    fate
My life wouldn't have been subject to this deplorable
    state
The snake of false prestige would not have bitten me
    with such hate
You are my son, were you to me less than a kingdom
    great?
I'd be happy were someone to set fire to this throne
    and crown
If you leave me, watch me if I don't burn this
    kingdom down.'

When the brave prince heard all at once his mother's
    piteous words
His heart felt as if it had been struck by a sword or
    worse

The moment was at hand when eyes would feel tears
    of remorse
But slowly in a level voice he began to converse
For he thought, she may not survive unless he held his
    peace
'My emotions will only cause her distress to increase.'

Then slowly he ventured to speak, and said, 'My
    mother dear
Please do control yourself, indeed for your well-being,
    I fear
I understand your sadness at this parting is severe
But do summon some patience, and this thought may
    bring some cheer
Perhaps this autumn is the way a new spring to instil
Maybe this is an expression of God's mysterious will.'

JIGAR MORADABADI

Jigar, ab maikade mein aa gaye ho to munaasib hai
Agar chupke se tum pee lo, musalmaan kaun dekhega?

Now that you are already in the tavern
It does behove you to indulge, dear Jigar
Quickly have a drink away from gazes stern
Here you are safe from the Muslim naysayer.

Ali Sikandar 'Jigar' Moradabadi (1890–1960) was an optician by trade. His work inaugurated the move of Urdu poetry toward the new century, which began as the century of servitude. Jigar's poetry reflects, perhaps, the initial response of Urdu poets—denial. His poetry retained the conventions of an earlier era, and he is best known for his exuberance in ghazals. The task of imbuing poetry with the sobering realism of its material and historical reality would be left to others, but Jigar continued to showcase his craft alongside them. His remarkable career continued right down to Independence and after. He was awarded the Sahitya Akademi Award by the Government of India in 1958, shortly before his death. He is also known to have mentored Majrooh Sultanpuri in his initial career.

The ghazal I have translated was sung by Abida Parveen, among others, and boasts two of the more popular shers of the twentieth century: the ones that begin '*Kya husn ne samjha hai*' and '*Ye ishq nahin aasaan*'.

EK LAFZ-E MOHABBAT

Ek lafz-e mohabbat ka, adna sa fasaana hai
Simte to dil-e aashiq, phaile to zamaana hai

Ye kis ka tasavvur hai, ye kis ka fasaana hai?
Jo ashk hai aankhon mein, tasbeeh ka daana hai

Hum ishq ke maaron ka itna hi fasaana hai
Rone ko nahin koi, hansne ko zamaana hai

Vo aur vafaa-dushman? Maanenge na maana hai
Sab dil ki sharaarat hai, aankhon ka bahaana hai

Kya husn ne samjha hai, kya ishq ne jaana hai
Hum khaak-nasheenon ki thokar mein zamaana hai

Vo husn-o-jamaal un ka ye ishq-o-shabaab apna
Jeene ki tamanna hai, marne ka zamaana hai

Ya vo thhe khafaa hum se, ya hum thhe khafaa un se
Kal un ka zamaana thha aaj apna zamaana hai

Ashkon ke tabassum mein, aahon ke tarannum mein
Maasoom mohabbat ka maasoom fasaana hai

Ye ishq nahin aasaan, itnaa to samajh leeje
Ek aag kaa dariya hai, aur doob ke jaana hai

Aansoo to bahut se hain, aankhon mein Jigar lekin
Bundh jaaye so moti hai, beh jaaye so daana hai

ONE WORD, LOVE

One word—love; when it shrinks, it can fit in a lover's
     heart
If it expands it is the whole and this world just a part

Whose imagination made a fable of this story?
Each teardrop in the eye is a bead of the rosary

We love-afflicted souls are cursed; the world enjoys
     our smile
This is our plight: if we cry, no one wants to stay awhile

Accuse not my love of infidelity! Not a chance!
Don't make much of mischievous eyes, and the heart's
     flirty glance

What has beauty understood, and what secrets has
     love known?
That the world is a captive of us dust-dwellers alone

His[1] beauty and grace against my love and youth
     collide
I want to live but truly it were better that I died

Was she unhappy with me, or was I upset with her?
The last time she was ascendant; this time is mine
     for sure

In the smile of teary eyes and in the rhythm of sighs
An innocent saga of innocent love, here it lies

It is not that easy to love, think before you desire
Do you have the gumption to swim across a sea of
    fire?

I have many tears in my eyes, what will become of
    them?
Either they'll be lost or, Jigar, they'll become pearls
    and gems.

FIRAAQ GORAKHPURI

Raghupati Sahay Firaaq Gorakhpuri (1896–1982) was one of the most prolific poets of his time. A professor of English at Allahabad University, he achieved the status of an organic intellectual, infusing his work with sensuality, and writing spiritedly in support of alternative sexualities in an atmosphere of heteronormativity. His 1936 article in defence of homosexual love and its depiction in the ghazal remains a classic, where he defiantly describes the depiction of homosexuality in poetry across time and cultures in the works of Sappho and Socrates, Saadi and Hafiz, Shakespeare and Whitman.[1] His well-known ghazal on forbidden and furtive love begins thus: '*Zara visaal ke baad aaina to dekh ai dost, / Tere Jamaal ki dosheezagi nazar aayi*' ('Look in the mirror after our union, friend / How your beauty has acquired a virgin innocence').

A fierce polemicist and a character who did not need any assistance in blowing his own trumpet, Firaaq wrote: '*Aane wali naslein tum par rashk karegi, hum-asro / Jab tum un se kahoge ye, hum ne Firaaq ko dekha thha*' ('Future generations will envy you, my dear peers / When you say unto them, I had seen Firaaq'). Firaaq was also a member of the Progressive Writers' Association, a spirited anti-colonialist, and enjoyed the confidence of Nehru and other early Congress functionaries.

His works appear in a number of anthologies, most published in the 1940s (the best known are *Shola-e Saaz* [The Fire of Rhythm], 1945, and *Shabnamistan* [Land of Dew], 1947). His essays were compiled in a book titled *Andaze* (Hunches). Firaaq won the Jnanpith Award (India's highest literary honour) in 1969, and remained the only Urdu poet Jnanpith awardee until Ali Sardar Jafri won it in 1997. Newcomers may have first encountered Firaaq's poetry through Jagjit Singh and Chitra Singh's rendition of '*Bahut pehle se un qadmon ki aahat jaan lete hain*' (We recognize those footsteps from a long way off), which they sang in the 1976 album *Unforgettables*.

I have chosen to translate just one of Firaaq's ghazals that, I feel, conjures a vivid sense of this remarkable poet.

SHAAM-E GHAM

Shaam-e gham kuchh us nigaah-e naaz ki baaten karo
Bekhudi badhti chali hai, raaz ki baaten karo

Nikhat-e zulf-e pareshaan, daastaan-e shaam-e gham
Subah hone tak isi andaz ki baaten karo

Ye sukoot-e yaas, ye dil ki ragon ka tootna
Khamoshi mein kuchh shikast-e saaz ki baaten karo

Kuchh qafas ki teeliyon se chhan rahaa hai noor sa
Kuchh fazaa kuchh hasrat-e parvaaz ki baatein karo

Jis ki furqat ne palat di ishq ki kaaya, Firaaq
Aaj usi Eesaa-nafas dum-saaz ki baaten karo

SAD EVENING

On this sad evening let us talk of the beloved's gaze
Let us talk of secret things for my passion is ablaze

The beauty of those tossed curls and the tale of this
    sad night
Till morning dawns, let us talk in such melancholic
    ways

In the silence of yearning, as hearts shatter, let us
    speak
How does it break, the instrument that such melodies
    plays?

From the bars of my prison, I feel a faint hint of light
Of my desire to spread my wings, let's talk about that
    phase

The one who has transformed the nature of my love,
    Firaaq
Let's talk of that Jesus-like lover who lights up my
    days.

JOSH MALIHABADI

Shabbir Hasan Khan 'Josh' Malihabadi (1898–1982) was the patron saint of the progressives, who conferred upon him the fond honorific *Shaayar-e Inquilab*—The Poet of the Revolution. He was a freedom-fighter, was close friends with Nehru, and was awarded the Padma Bhushan in 1952. He migrated to Pakistan in 1958, ostensibly to serve Urdu (and to escape the complications that arose from some extramarital affairs with the spouses of powerful people, if his wild autobiography is to be believed), but was generally shunned by the Establishment for his leftist views. He continued to write prolifically; he published seven poetry collections, the most popular being *Shola-o-Shabnam* (Flame and Dew). Josh was also a skilful exponent of the marsiya: the website http://urdushahkar.org contains five marsiyas of Josh, duly translated, transliterated, annotated and declaimed by S.M. Shahed.

In his autobiography *Yaadon ki Baraat* (The Procession of Memories—itself a marvel of embellished anecdote), Josh describes a moment in 1939 when he heard a speech on radio delivered by the British governor of Lucknow, which urged Indians to join the Allied effort against the Axis, for that was the only way 'to save humanity from that barbarian, Hitler.' An incensed Josh claims that he wrote a poem (translated below), titled '*East India Company ke Farzandon se Kalaam*' ('Address to the Heirs of the East India Company') in fifteen minutes. He had to suffer the consequences of his action, but escaped jail because the freedom movement was in full swing and had already stretched the incarcerating capacity of the British rulers. Josh was instead placed under house arrest.

EAST INDIA COMPANY KE FARZANDON SE KALAAM

Kis zuban se keh rahe ho aaj ai saudagaro
'Dahr mein insaniyat ke naam ko ooncha karo
Jis ko sab kahte hain Hitler, bhedia hai bhedia
Bhediye ko mar do goli pa-ye amn-o-baqa
Baghe insani mein chalne hi ko hai baad-e khizan
Aadmiyat le rahi hai hichkiyon pe hichkiyan
Hath Hitlar ka hai rakhsh-e khudsari ki bag par
Tegh ka pani chidak do Germany ki aag par.'

Sakht hairan hoon ke mehfil mein tumhari aur ye zikr
Nau-e insani ke mustaqbil ki ab karte ho fikr!
Jab yahan aaye thhe tum saudagari ke vaaste
Nau-e insani ke mustaqbil se kiya vaqif na thhe?
Hindiyon ke jism mein, kya rooh-e aazadi na thhi?
Sach batao, kya voh insanon ki aabadi na thhi?

Apne zulm-e be-nehayat ka fasaana yaad hai?
Company ka bhi voh daur-e mujrimana yaad hai?
Loot-te phirte thhe tum, jab karvan dar karvan
Sar-barhana phir rahi thhi daulat-e Hindustan
Dast-karon ke angoothey kaat-te phirte thhe tum!
Sard lashon se gadhon ko paat-te phirte thhe tum!
Sanat-e Hindustan par, maut thhi chhayi hui
Maut bhi kaisi? Tumhare haath ki layi hui!

Allah Allah, kis qadar insaaf ke talib ho aaj
Mir Jafar ki qasam, kya dushman-e haq thha Siraj?
Voh Avadh ki begamon ka bhi satana yaad hai?
Yaad hai, Jhansi ki rani ka zamaana yaad hai?
Hijrat-e sultan-e Dilli ka samaa bhi yaad hai?
Sher-dil Tipu ki khooni dastaan bhi yaad hai?
Teesre faaqe mein ek girte hue ko thaam-ne
Kin ke sar laaye thhe tum Shah-Zafar ke saamne?
Yaad to hogi voh Mityaburj ki bhi dastan?
Ab bhi jis ki khaak se reh-reh ke uthta hai dhuan
Tum ne Qaisar Bagh ko dekha to hoga bar-ha?
Aaj bhi aati hai jis se 'Haay Akhtar' ki sada
Such kaho kya hafize mein hai voh zulm-e be-panah
Aaj tak Rangoon mein ek qabr jis ki hai gavah
Zehn mein hoga yeh taaza Hindiyon ka Dagh bhi
Yaad to hoga tumhe Jalianwala Bagh bhi?
Poochh lo us se tumhara naam kyon ta-banda hai
Dyer-e garg-e dahan aalood ab bhi zinda hai
Voh Bhagat Singh, ab bhi jis ke gham mein dil
nashaad hai
Us ki gardan mein jo dala tha voh phanda yaad ha?
Hind ki rahbar rahaa karte thhe kis sanjaar se
Poochh lo ye qaidkhanon ke dar-o-deevar se
Ab bhi hai mahfooz jis me tantana sarkar ka
Aaj bhi goonji hui hai jin mein kodon ki sada

Aaj kashti, khulq ke amwaj par khetey ho kyun?
Sakht hairan hoon ke ab tum dars-e haq dete ho kyun
Ahl-e quvvat daam-e haq mein to kabhi aate nahin
Aadmiyat ko kabhi khatir hi mein latay nahin?

Lekin aaj akhlaq ki talqeen farmate ho tum
Ho na ho apne mein ab quvvat nahin pate ho tum

'Ahl-e haq roshan-nazar hain, ahl-e batil kor hain'
Yeh to hain aqwaal un qaumon ke jo kamzor hain
Aaj shayad, manzil-e quvvat me tum rahte nahin
'Jis ki lathi us ki bhains' ab kis liye kahte nahin?

Der se baithey ho, nakhl-e rasti ki chaoun mein
Kiya, khuda-na-kardah, kuchh moch aa gayee hai
paon mein?
Goonj tapon ki na aabadi, na veerane mein hai
Khair to hai? Asp-e taazi kya shifakhane me hai?
Aaj kal to har nazar mein, rahm ka andaz hai
Kuchh tabiyat kya naseeb-e dushmanan naa-saaz hai?
Sans kiya ukhdi, ke haq ke naam par marne lagey!
Nau-e insan ki hawa khawahi ka dam bharne lagey!
Zulm bhoole, ragini insaf ki gane lagey
Lag gayi hai aag kya ghar mein ke chillane lagey?

Mujrimon ke vaaste zeba nahin yeh shor-o-shain
Kal Yazid-o-Shimr thhe, aur aaj bante ho Husain
Khair, ai saudagaro, ab hai to bus is baat mein
Waqt ke farmaan ke aage jhuka do gardanen
Ek kahani waqt likhega naye mazmoon ki
Jis ki surkhi ko zaroorat hai tumhare khoon ki
Waqt ka farmaan apna rukh badal sakta nahin
Maut tal sakti hai ye farmaan tal sakta nahin.

ADDRESS TO THE HEIRS OF THE EAST INDIA COMPANY

With what tongues can you say this, dear traders?
'Do your bit to exalt the name of humanity in this
    world
The one they call Hitler is a wolf, no more than a wolf
Let us shoot the wolf in the name of peace and sanity

The garden of humanity is now beset by autumn
Humanity languishes in thirst and yearning while
Hitler's hand grasps the mane of the steed
Throw the water of the sword on Germany's fire.'

Amazed am I at such talk in your gathering
Now you think of the future of humanity
When you came here as shopkeepers, to ply your trade
Were you not aware of the future of humanity then?
Did the Indians not harbour the soul of freedom in
      their bodies?
Speak the truth—was it not a congregation of humans?

Do you even remember the story of your unparalleled
      tyranny
And of the [East India] Company's reign of terror
When you went about looting caravan after caravan
And the wealth of India scurried about bareheaded?
You used to go about cutting off the hands of weavers
And filling holes in the ground with cold corpses
The industry of India had death all over it
And what a death? One brought about by you!

Allah Allah! Now you seek justice?
Tell us in the name of Mir Jafar, was Siraj[1] an enemy
      of truth?
Remember you, harassing the ladies of Avadh?
Do you remember that Rani of Jhansi?
Can you recall the migration of the King of Delhi
And the bloody history of the lionhearted Tipu?
And to help the person tottering on his third day of
      fasting
Whose heads did you place in front of King Zafar?[2]

Do you remember the story of Metiaburj[3]
Even now its dust is redolent with smoke
You must have seen Qaiser Bagh many a time
Where, even now, a dirge to Akhtar echoes
Tell me, does your memory encompass that tyranny
Of which a grave in Rangoon bears witness?
Recall you, that still raw wound in Indian hearts
This is called Jalianwala Bagh, remember?
Ask it why you are so well remembered here
For Dyer, the bloody fanged, is still alive[4]
That Bhagat Singh, in whose memory the heart is still
    unhappy
The noose you put around his neck, do you not
    remember that?
The leaders of India lived in such penury
Ask that of the doors and walls of your dungeons
Where, even now, your governance is remembered
And the sound of the whip still echoes.

Now suddenly, your boat is being docked on the
    banks of civility
To my amazement, you have begun to preach about
    truth
The folks in power hardly ever speak of who is right
And bringing humanity into the conversation is not
    your style

Yet, now you counsel us to be forgiving
Sure enough, you must have lost your strength
'Those who are on the right are wise, and those who
    are ignorant are cruel'
This is usually the talk of the defeated!

Perhaps you are no longer in a powerful position
Hence you do not chant, 'He who owns the stick
    owns the cow.'

For a while now, you have been sitting in the shade of
    a different path
Are you okay sir, or is your foot a bit sprained?
There is no sound of hooves here, nor in the
    wilderness
Is your fleet steed ill, at the hospital; is all well?
Nowadays, every gaze of yours is full of tenderness
Sure all is well, or is the fortune of mine enemy a bit
    troubled?
Your breath seems laboured, and so you have turned
    moral
And speak of sojourns into the strange path of
    humanity
Now you feel tyranny, so you speak of justice
Why do you scream so, is your house on fire today?

It does not behove criminals to be indignant
Till yesterday, you were Yazid and Shimr, and today,
    you want to be Husain[5]?
Anyway, shopkeepers, this is what needs to be done:
That you bow down before the verdict of destiny
Time will write a new story, with a new title
And this story needs to be reddened with your
    blood.
The verdict of time cannot be made to change course
Death may wait, but this verdict awaits no one.

MAKHDOOM MOHIUDDIN

Hayaat le ke chalo, kaayenaat le ke chalo
Chalo to saare zamaane ko saath le ke chalo

Carry life as you walk, and carry the firmament too
Walk so, that the entire world should choose to walk with
    you

Abu Sayeed Mohammad Makhdoom Mohiuddin Huzri (1908–69)
lived in the city of the famous Charminar, and is lovingly known
as the fifth minar of Hyderabad. Born into poverty, he grew up
sweeping mosque courtyards, but soon became a trade union
leader. He was a member of the Communist Party of India,
and even represented it in the state assembly. He was one of
the architects of the 1946–47 Telangana Rebellion against the
government of the nizam of Hyderabad. His poem *'Telangana'*
was an anthem for the movement, and continued to be deployed
during the struggle for statehood by Telangana in independent
India. Much in the fashion of Vladimir Mayakovsky, the Russian
poet who had influenced him, Makhdoom struggled against his
tendencies to wax metaphysical, choosing to eschew finer verbal
constructions in the service of anthems and group songs, which
unthinking literary critics often interpret as simplistic.

I have translated three poems below, the latter two of which
are to be read as a series. The first, *'Intezaar'* ('The Wait') is an

exposition of Makhdoom's gentle lyricism.[1] The other two poems are much more strident, programmatic, with simple rhythms, reflecting their status as chants and songs. The first, an anti-war piece, was composed by Makhdoom in the early 1930s, when Indians were being forcibly conscripted by the British to fight in the Second World War. It was sung by Kumar Sanu for Ali Sardar Jafri's TV serial on progressive poets, *Kahkashan*, and was also featured in the 1960 film *Usne Kaha Thha*. However, Makhdoom's attitude to the war became much more positive once the Soviet Union joined it following Hitler's infamous Operation Barbarossa in 1941. Like many leftists of that time, he saw the war now as a part of a broader struggle against imperialism, rather than a fight between two foreign powers. His song '*Jang-e Aazadi*' reflected his new sentiments.

1   INTEZAAR

> *Raat bhar deeda-e namnaak mein lehraate rahe*
> *Saans ki tarah se aap aate rahe, jaate rahe*
>
> *Khush thhe ham apni tamannaon ka khwaab aayegaa*
> *Apna armaan bar-afganda naqaab aayegaa*
> *Nazarein neechee kiye sharmaaye huwe aayegaa*
> *Kaakulein chehre pe bikhraaye huwe aayegaa*
>
> *Aa gayi thi dil-e muztar mein shakeebaai si*
> *Baj rahi thi mere gham-khaane mein shehnaai si*
>
> *Shab ke jaage huwe taaron ko bhi neend aane lagi*
> *Aap ke aane ki ik aas thi, ab jaane lagi*
>
> *Subah ne sej se uth-te huwe li angdaai*
> *Ai sabaa, tu bhi jo aayi to akele aayi*

Mere mehboob meri neend udaane vaale
Mere masjood meri rooh pe chhaane vaale
Aa bhi jaataa, ke mere sajdon ka armaan nikle
Aa bhi jaataa, tere qadmon pe meri jaan nikle

THE WAIT

All night, in my moist eyes you continued to sway
Like my breath, you kept coming and going away

I was happy, that the dream of my desires would
    come
My shy lover, encased in a veil, eyes downcast, would
    come
Inciting my passion with hair strewn over face, would
    come

My impatient heart had achieved contentment and
    belief
A *shehnai* struck up, and sadness gave way to relief

But soon, the stars, which had stayed awake all night,
    nodded off
The hope of your arrival gave way to a cynic's scoff

The morning eventually woke up; a new sun shone
O morning breeze, you did come, but alas, you came
    alone

Enchanted lover mine, who stole the sleep from my
    sad eyes

I bowed to you, you ruled my dreams, now I'm
    shamed by those lies
Would that my prayers would bear fruit, and we
    would meet
Would that you'd come and I'd breathe my last at
    your feet.

2   JAANE VAALE SIPAHI SE POOCHHO

Jaane vaale sipahi se poochho
Vo kahaan ja raha hai?

Ishq hai haasil-e zindagaani
Khoon se tar hai uski javaani
Hai maasoom bachpan ki yaaden
Hai do roz ki nau-javaani

Jaane vaale sipahi se poochho
Vo kahaan ja raha hai?

Kaun dukhiya hai jo gaa rahi hai?
Bhookhe bachhon ko behla rahi hai
Lash jalne ki bu aa rahi hai
Zindagi hai ke chilla rahi hai

Jaane vaale sipahi se poochho
Vo kahaan ja raha hai?

Kitne sehme hue hain nazaare
Kaisa dar dar ke chalte hain taare
Kya javaani ka khoon ho raha hai?
Surkh hai aanchalon ke kinaare

Jaane vaale sipahi se poochho
Vo kahaan ja raha hai?

Hil raha hai siyaahi ka dera
Ho raha hai meri jaan savera
O vatan chhod ke jaane waale
Khul gaya inquilaabi pharera

Jaane vaale sipahi se poochho
Vo kahaan ja raha hai?

ASK THAT DEPARTING SOLDIER

Ask that departing soldier
Where he is headed

A well-spent life leads to love eternal
But this story's fate is to be writ in blood
He harbours memories of an innocent childhood
But his youth is destined to be ephemeral.

Ask that departing soldier
Where he is headed

Who is that sad woman who is singing?
She is comforting her hungry children
The air stings and reeks as a corpse burns
And what of life? It is screaming

Ask that departing soldier
Where he is headed

Why are these vistas so fearful?
Why do the stars move with such dread?
Is youth being murdered here?
The borders of clothing are blood red

But look now, the darkness is lifting
My dear, see the colour of dawn
O departing soldier, hang on
The revolutionary banner's unfurling

Ask that departing soldier
Where he is headed.

3   JANG-E AAZADI

Ye jang hai jang-e aazadi
Aazadi ke parcham ke tale

Hum Hind ke rehne waalon ki
Mazdooron ka dehqaanon ki
Aazadi ke matwaalon ki
Dehqanon ki, mazdooron ki

Ye jang hai jang-e aazadi
Aazadi ke parcham ke tale

Saara sansaar hamaara hai
Poorab, Pachhim, Uttar Dakshin
Hum Afrangi, hum Amreeki
Hum Cheeni jaanbaazaan-e watan
Hum surkh sipaahi, zulm-shikan
Aahan paikar, faulaad badan

Ye jang hai jang-e aazadi
Aazadi ke parcham ke tale

Lo surkh savera aata hai
Aazadi ka, aazadi ka
Gulnaar taraana gaata hai
Aazadi ka, aazadi ka
Dekho parcham lehraata hai
Aazadi ka, aazadi ka

Ye jang hai jang-e aazadi
Aazadi ke parcham ke tale

THE WAR FOR FREEDOM

This war is the war for freedom
Fought under the banner of freedom

The war for all Indians
The labourers and the farmers
The lovers of freedom
The farmers and the labourers

This war is the war for freedom
Under the banner of freedom

The whole world is ours
The East and the West, the North and the South
We Europeans, we Americans
We Chinese soldiers of our homeland
We, the red soldiers, the crushers of tyranny
Torsos like the furnace, bodies like steel

This war is the war for freedom
Under the banner of freedom

Behold, the red dawn arrives
Of freedom, of freedom
It sings the flower-red song
Of freedom, of freedom
Look, the banner waves in the sky
Of freedom, of freedom

This war is the war for freedom
Fought under the banner of freedom.

MAJAZ

Is mehfil-e kaif-o-masti mein, is anjuman-e irfani mein
Sab jaam-bakaf baithe hi rahe, hum pi bhi gaye, chhalka
bhi gaye

In this celebratory gathering, in the company of wisdom
Everyone kept holding his glass; I drank my fill, even spilled
   some.

Asrar-ul Haq Majaz (1909–55) emerged in the heady academic
atmosphere of Aligarh in the 1930s, and was quite the rock star
in university circles. Flamboyantly dedicating his poetry to social
change, he never could renounce his innate romanticism. The
resultant output was truly an exemplar of the best offerings of
progressive Urdu poetry. Majaz's spirited critique of patriarchy
made him quite the cynosure of rebel Muslim female eyes. His
poems critiquing the institution of purdah (for instance, '*koi aur*
shai hai, ye ismat nahin hai'; 'whatever it is, this is not virtue')
are a very significant part of his poetry, as are his existential
verses, presaging the anomie and loneliness that emerge from
the hegemony of industrial capital. Majaz's early death has also
added a layer of youthfulness to his mystique.

I have translated three poems here. The first is an excerpt
from a lyrical tribute to a train, hardly the most romantic of

subjects until it fell into Majaz's deft hands.[1] To Majaz, a train was the ultimate symbol of progressive modernity, all steel and straight lines, cutting purposively through nature. The second is Majaz's despairing depiction of urban alienation, which is perhaps his best-known poem and also appeared as a song in the 1948 film *Thokar*. The third, '*Khwab-e Sahar*'('Dream of Dawn'), is a remarkable repudiation of religiosity that showcases the emerging rejection of spirituality by progressive poets and casts religion as a barrier to human progress and emancipation. It was written in 1936; one can only estimate the reception it would have garnered in present times.

1   **RAAT AUR RAIL**[2]

> *Phir chali hai rail, istayshan se lehraati hui*
> *Neem shab ki khamushi mein zer-e lab gaati hui*
>
> *Daalti behis chattaanon par hiqaarat ki nazar*
> *Koh par hansti, falak ko aankh dikhlaati hui*
>
> *Daaman-e taariki-e shab ki udaati dhajjiyaan*
> *Qasr-e zulmat par musalsal teer barsaati hui*
>
> *Zad mein koi cheez aa jaaye to us ko pees kar*
> *Irteqaa-e zindagi ke raaz batlaati hui*
>
> *Al-gharaz, badhti chali jaati hai, be khauf-o-khatar*
> *Shaayar-e aatish-nafas ka khoon khaulaati hui*

THE NIGHT AND THE TRAIN

Once again, the train jauntily leaves the station
Breaking the silence of the night with its whispered
song.

Casting scornful glances on the placid cliffs
Laughing at mountains, making eyes at the sky.

Tearing the black fabric of the night into smithereens
Shooting constant arrows of sparks at the palace of
darkness.

Crushing anything that comes in its way
Revealing the secrets of the evolution of life.

Ultimately it flies, fearlessly,
Roiling the blood of the fire-souled poet.

2　**AAWARA**

Shahr ki raat aur main naashaad-o-naakaara phirun
Jagmagaati jaagti sadkon pe aawara phirun
Ghair ki basti hai, kab tak darbadar maraa phirun
Ai gham-e dil kya karun, ai vahshat-e dil, kya karun

Jhilmilaate qumqumon ki raah mein zanjeer si
Raat ke hathon mein din ki mohini tasveer si
Mere seene par magar dahki hui shamsheer si
Ai gham-e dil kya karun, ai vahshat-e dil, kya karun

Majaz 139

Ye roopahli chhaon, ye aakash par taaron ka jaal
Jaise Sufi ka tasavvur, jaise aashiq ka khayaal
Aah lekin kaun jaane, kaun samjhe ji ka haal
Ai gham-e dil kya karun, ai vahshat-e dil, kya karun

Phir vo toota ek sitara, phir vo chhooti phuljhadi
Jaane kiski god mein aayi hai moti ki ladi
Hook si seene mein uthi, chot si dil par padi
Ai gham-e dil kya karun, ai vahshat-e dil, kya karun

Raat hans hans kar ye kehti hai ke maikhaane mein
      chal
Phir kisi Shahnaz-e la'ala rukh ke kaashaane mein
      chal
Ye nahin mumkin to phir ai dost, veerane mein chal
Ai gham-e dil kya karun, ai vahshat-e dil, kya karun

Har taraf bikhri hui rangeeniyan ra'anaaiyan
Har qadam par ishraten leti hui angdaaiyan
Badh rahi hai god phailaye hue rusvaaiyan
Ai gham-e dil kya karun, ai vahshat-e dil, kya karun

Raaste mein ruk ke dam le loon meri aadat nahin
Laut kar vaapas chalaa jaoon, meri fitrat nahin
Aur koi ham-navaa mil jaaye ye qismat nahin
Ai gham-e dil kya karun, ai vahshat-e dil, kya karun

Muntazir hai ek toofan-e balaa mere liye
Ab bhi jaane kitne darwaaze hain vaa mere liye
Par museebat hai mera ahd-e vafaa mere liye
Ai gham-e dil kya karun, ai vahshat-e dil, kya karun

Jee mein aata hai ke ab ahd-e vafaa bhi tod doon
Un ko paa sakta hoon main, ye aasra bhi tod doon
Haan, munaasib hai ke zanjeer-e vafaa bhi tod doon
Ai gham-e dil kya karun, ai vahshat-e dil, kya karun

Ek mahal ki aad se niklaa vo peela maahtab
Jaise mulla ka amaama, jaise baniye ki kitab
Jaise muflis ki javaani, jaise bevaa ka shabab
Ai gham-e dil kya karun, ai vahshat-e dil, kya karun

Dil mein ek shola bhadak utha hai, aakhir kya karoon
Mera paimana chhalak utha hai, aakhir kya karoon
Zakhm seene ka mehak utha hai, aakhir kya karoon
Ai gham-e dil kya karun, ai vahshat-e dil, kya karun

Jee mein aata hai, ye murda chand taare noch loon
Is kinaare noch loon, aur us kinaare noch loon
Ek do ka zikr kya, saare ke saare noch loon
Ai gham-e dil kya karun, ai vahshat-e dil, kya karun

Muflisi, aur ye manaazir hain nazar ke saamne
Saikdon sultan-o-jaabir hain nazar ke samne
Saikdon Changez-o-Nadir hain nazar ke saamne
Ai gham-e dil kya karun, ai vahshat-e dil, kya karun

Le ke ek Changez ke haathon se khanjar tod doon
Taj par us ke damakta hai jo patthar tod doon
Koi tode ya na tode, main hi badh kar tod doon
Ai gham-e dil kya karun, ai vahshat-e dil, kya karun

Badh ke is Indarsabha ka saaz-o-saaman phoonk doon
Is ka gulshan phoonk doon, us ka shabistan phoonk
    doon

*Takht-e sultan kya, main saara qasr-e sultan phoonk
    doon*
Ai gham-e dil kya karun, ai vahshat-e dil, kya karun

VAGABOND

Night has fallen in the city, and I, unhappy and
    defeated
Roam, a vagabond on dazzling, awake streets
It is not my neighbourhood, how long can I loiter
    thus?
Anguished heart, desperate heart, what should I do?

In the glittering sky, the streetlights seem linked in a
    chain
The bosom of the night holds the image of a beautiful
    day
But the lights fall on my heart like the flash of a
    scimitar
Anguished heart, desperate heart, what should I do?

These beautiful shadows, this net of stars on the sky
Like a Sufi's contemplation, a poet's thought
But ah, who is to know, to understand, a soul's
    plight?
Anguished heart, desperate heart, what should I do?

There falls a shooting star, like a sparkler
A string of pearls fell in somebody's lap, perhaps?
Desolation rises in my chest, hitting the heart like a
    blow
Anguished heart, desperate heart, what should I do?

The night laughs gaily, and invites me to a tavern
'Or come then, to the boudoir of a rose-cheeked beauty
If not, then join me, my friend, among the ruins'
Anguished heart, desperate heart, what should I do?

Bright colours and lovely images lie scattered
At every step, joys beckon languorously
But look here, sorrows and defeats also proffer their
    laps
Anguished heart, desperate heart, what should I do?

To stop and rest on the way is not my habit
To admit defeat and return is not in my nature
But to find a companion, alas, is not my fate
Anguished heart, desperate heart, what should I do?

A storm of misfortune lies, ready to waylay me
And though several open doors still beckon me
An old promise of fealty holds me back, like a curse
Anguished heart, desperate heart, what should I do?

Sometimes I wonder: should I break those foolish vows?
Should I even surrender the hope that love will be rewarded?
It is possible, is it not, that I could break this feeble chain?
Anguished heart, desperate heart, what should I do?

From behind a palace, emerges the yellow moon
Like a mullah's turban, like a moneylender's ledger
Like a poor man's youth, a widow's beauty
Anguished heart, desperate heart, what should I do?

My heart burns like a flame, what should I do?
The cup of my patience brims over, what should I do?

The wound in my chest is fragrant, what should I do?
Anguished heart, desperate heart, what should I do?

I want to pluck this dead moon, these dead stars from
      the sky
Pluck them from this end of the horizon and from
      that corner
What is one or two, I want to pluck them all out
Anguished heart, desperate heart, what should I do?

These beautiful sights mock my helpless poverty
Hundreds of wealthy kings profane my gaze
Hundreds of Chengizes, hundreds of Nadirs to behold[3]
Anguished heart, desperate heart, what should I do?

Ah that I could break every sword in the hands of
      every Chengiz
Pull out the diadem from his crown and break it too
Why wait for anyone else, let me break it myself
Anguished heart, desperate heart, what should I do?

Walk into the Indrasabha[4] and burn it to the ground,
Burn down their garden, and burn down their bedchamber!
Not just the crown, I should burn the entire palace!
Anguished heart, desperate heart, what should I do?

3   KHWAB-E SAHAR

Mahr sadiyon se chamakta hi raha aflaak par
Raat hi taari rahi insaan ke idraak par
Aql ke maidaan mein zulmat ka dera hi raha
Dil mein taareeki, dimaghon mein andhera hi raha

Ik na ik mazhab ki sai khaam bhi hoti rahi
Ahl-e dil par barish-e ilhaam bhi hoti rahi
Masjidon mein maulvi khutbe sunaate hi rahe
Mandiron mein barahman ashlok gaate hi rahe

Aadmi minnat kash-e arbaab-e irfaan hi raha
Dard-e insani magar mahroom-e darmaan hi raha

Ik na ik dar par jabeen-e shauq ghisti hi rahi
Aadmiyat zulm ki chakki mein pisti hi rahi
Rahbari jaari rahi, paighambari jaari rahi
Deen ke parde mein jang-o-zargari jaari rahi
Ye musalsal aafaten, ye yoorishen, ye qatl-e aam
Aadmi kab tak rahe auham-e batil ka ghulam
Zahn-e insani ne ab auhaam ke zulmaat mein
Zindagi ki sakht toofani andheri raat mein

Kuchh nahin to kam se kam khwab-e sahar dekha to hai
Jis taraf dekha na tha ab tak, udhar dekha to hai

THE DREAM OF DAWN

The sun did shine as bright as always in the
    firmament
Yet over the human mind the dark did not relent
Darkness pitched its opaque camp amid the fields of mind
Lightlessness now ruled the hearts, intellect was
    rendered blind
By turns, a different religion established its reign
And its wisdom fell upon believers just like rain
Maulvis made fiery speeches in mosques at all times
While in temples, the Brahmins chanted their holy rhymes

Humanity continued its leaders to beseech
A cure for its angst, alas, remained out of its reach

Foreheads bent at holy thresholds, supplicants stayed
    prone
Yet humans remained crushed by tyrannical
    grindstones
Pious leaders preached and the prophetic game
    prospered
War and accumulation, in religion's name prospered
These continuous calamities, massacres, assaults
Should humans remain enslaved in superstition's
    vaults?
In these black and stormy days of false faith and belief
In this dark night of life, humanity craves relief

If nothing else, we have at least dared to dream of dawn
That which we'd never glimpsed, to that place our
    gaze has gone.

N.M. RASHID

Raja Nazar Mohammed Janjua (1910–75) preferred to be
known as Noon Meem Rashid. He will also be known as a true
exponent of the modernist craft and a master of Urdu free verse.
He published four volumes of poetry, each with a wonderful title.
They were *Maavra* (Beyond), *Iran mein Ajnabi* (A Stranger in
Iran), *La Musawi Insan* (Nothingness = Human) and *Guman
ka Mumkin* (The Possibility of Doubt).

Rashid worked for the United Nations, lived in England, and
willed that his body be cremated. These disparate demographic
details offer glimpses of the life of a modernist. In his poetry, he
was especially contemptuous of the ghazal, choosing to free his
words from rhyme, metre, linearity and social commentary. His
poems dredge up from the subconscious a vibrant spectrum of
individual ideas—quite unique in their time, but often imitated
later by a growing army of acolytes.

Rashid's poems do not lend themselves to easy interpretation,
and I would not recommend them to the neophyte reader without
some serious handholding.[1] The poem I have translated below
is the first part of an extended poem (Rashid wrote it in four
discrete parts; each can be read on its own, or as part of a series).
The story in brief involves an Iraqi potter named Hasan, who
falls madly in love with a mysterious beauty called Jahanzad.
Hasan's passion induces in him a nine-year period of insanity
that causes him to become distant from his craft. In a moment of

relative lucidity, he encounters Jahanzad again, and unapologetic about his affliction, suggests that he may become the potter of old again, but only if his love is requited. It is a strange story of desire and creativity, of sanity and madness, and also represents the best traditions of the Urdu aazad nazm (free verse poem), where relaxing the strictures of rhyme and metre do not absolve the poet of the imperatives of rhythm.

HASAN KOOZAGAR

Jahanzad, neeche gali mein tere dar ke aage
Ye main sokhta sar, Hasan Koozagar hoon!

Tujhe subha bazaar mein boodhe attar Yusuf
Ki dukkan par main ne dekha
To teri nigaahon mein vo taabnaaki
Thhi main jin ki hasrat mein nau saal deevana phirta
 raha hoon

Jahanzad, nau saal deevana phirta raha hoon!
Ye woh daur tha jis me main ne
Kabhi apne ranjoor koozon ki jaanib
Palat kar na dekha . . .
Woh kooze, mere dast-e chabuk ke putle
Gil-o-rang-o-raughan ki makhlooq-e bejaan
Woh sargoshion mein ye kehte:
'Hasan Koozagar ab kahan hai?
Woh hum se, khud apne amal se
Khudawand ban kar khudaaon ki manind hai rooy-e
 gardaan!'

Jahanzad, nau saal ka daur yoon mujh pe guzra
Ke jaise kisi shehr-e madfoon par waqt guzre.
Taghaaron mein mitti
Kabhi jis ki khushboo se waarafta hota tha main
        Sang-basta padi thi
Suraahi-o-meena-o-jam-o-suboo aur faanoos-o-guldaan
Meri hech-maya ma'eeshat ke, izhaar-e fan ke sahaare
        Shikasta pade the.

Main khud, main Hasan Koozagar, pa-ba gil, khaak
        bar-sar, barahna
Sar-e chaak zhooleeda-moonh, sar ba-zaanu
Kisi gham-zada devta ki tarah waaheme ke
Gil-o-la se khaabon ke sayyal kooze banata raha tha

Jahanzad, nau saal pehle
Tu naadan thi lekin tujhe ye khabar thi
Ke main ne, Hasan Koozagar ne
Teri qaaf ki si ufaq taab aankhon mein dekhi hai vo
        taabnaaki
Ke jis se mere jism-o-jaan, abr-o-mahtaab ka
Rahguzar ban gaye the

Jahanzad, Baghad ki khaab goon raat
Vo rood-e Dajla ka saahil
Vo kashti, vo mallah ki band aankhen
Kisi khasta-jaan, ranj-bar koozagar ke liye
Ek hi raat vo kahrbaa thi
Ke jis se abhi tak hai paiwast us ka wajood,
Us ki jaan, us ka paikar
Magar ek hi raat ka zauq darya ki vo lehr nikla
Hasan Koozagar jis mein dooba to ubhra nahin hai!

Jahanzad, is daur mein roz, har roz
Vo sokhta bakht aa kar
Mujhe dekhti chaak par paa-ba-gil, sar-ba-zaanu
To shaanon se mujh ko hilaati . . .
(wahi chaak jo saal-haa saal jeene ka tanhaa sahaara
     raha tha!)
Vo shaanon se mujh ko hilaati:
'Hasan Koozagar, hosh mein aa
Hasan apne veeran ghar par nazar kar
Ye bachchon ke tannoor kyon-kar bharenge?
Hasan, ai mohabbat ke mare,
Mohabbat ameeron ki baazi
Hasan apne deevar-o-dar par nazar kar'
Mere kaan mein ye nawa-e hazeen yoon thi jaise
Kisi doobte shakhs ko zer-e gardaab koi pukaare!
Vo askhon ke ambaar phoolon ke ambaar thhe, haan
Magar main, Hasan Koozagar, shehr-e auhaam ke un
Kharaabon ka mahjoor tha jis
Mein koi sadaa, koi jumbish
Kisi murgh-e parran ka saaya
Kisi zindagi ka nishaan tak nahin tha!

Jahanzad, main aaj teri gali mein
Yahaan, raat ki sard-goon teergi mein
Tere dar ke aage khada hoon
Sar-o-mu pareshaan
Dareeche se vo qaaf ki si tilismi nigaahen
Mujhe aaj phir jhaankti hain
Zamaana, Jahanzad, vo chaak hai jis pe meena-o-
     jam-o-subu
Aur faanoos-o-guldaan
Ke maanind bante bigadte hain insaan

Main insaan hoon lekin
Ye nau saal jo gham ke qaalib mein guzre!
Hasan Koozagar aaj ek tauda-e khaak hai jis
Mein nam ka asar tak nahin hai

Jahanzad, bazaar mein subha attar Yusuf
Ki dukkan par teri aankhen
Phir ek baar kuchh keh gayi hain
Un aankhon ki taabinda shokhi
Se uthi hai phir tauda-e khaak mein nam ki halki si
      larzish
Yahi shaayad is khaak ko gil bana de!

Tamanna ki wus'at ki kis ko khabar hai, Jahanzad, lekin
Tu chaahe to ban jaoon main phir
Wahi koozagar jis ke kooze
Thhe har kaakh-o-ku aur har shehr-o-qariya ki naazish
Thhe jin se ameer-o-gada ke masaakin darakhshaan
Tamanna ki wus'at ki kis ko khabar hai, Jahanzad, lekin
Tu chahe to main phir palat jaoon un apne mehjoor
      koozon ki jaanib
Gil-o-la ke sookhe taghaaron ki jaanib
Ma'eeshat ke, izhaar-e fan ke sahaaron ki jaanib
Ke main us gil-o-la se, us rang-o-raughan
Se phir vo sharaare nikaaloon
Ke jin se dilon ke kharaabe hon roshan!

HASAN THE POTTER

Jahanzad, in the street below, just ahead of your
      house
I stand with heart aflame, Hasan the potter.

In the morning I saw you in the shop of that old
    perfumer, Yousuf
And your eyes had the same passion
The desire for which committed me to nine years of
    madness.

Jahanzad, nine years of insanity!
That was the time when I
Cast not another look at my spurned pots
Those pots, statues enslaved by my creative whip
Lifeless creations of clay, colour and grease
They would speak in whispers
'Where is Hasan the potter?
He has distanced himself from us, from his labour, and
Like gods, he has become invisible.'

Jahanzad, those nine years happened to me
Like time happens to ruins, to buried cities
The dust in the flowerpots
Whose fragrance once enamoured me
Lay under stones
Goblet and cup and chandelier and lantern and vase
The artefacts through which I expressed my existence,
    my art
Lay broken

Me, myself, Hasan the potter, immobile as a tree
A dusty face in front of the wheel, head bowed
Lay there like a sad deity
And with the clay and the nothingness of doubts, I
    made pots of empty dreams.

Jahanzad, nine years ago,
You were innocent, but I'm sure you knew

That I, Hasan the potter, had seen
In your bright eyes, like the mystical mountain of
        Caucasus
Such heat, such passion
That my body and soul had become
The wayfarers of clouds and the moon.

Remember Jahanzad, that dreamy Baghdad night
The banks of the Tigris
The boat, the closed eyes of the boatman
I tell you that for a tired, disheartened potter
That one night was such a maelstrom
That even now, his being, his life, his body
Remain associated with them
But the passion of one night of turned into such a
        tidal wave
That Hasan the potter, once he went under, has not
        surfaced yet.

Jahanzad, in those days, every day
That unlucky wife of mine would come
Find me on the wheel immobile, bowed of head
(The same wheel that had been our sole means of
        support for years)
And she would shake me by the shoulder
Gently she would shake me
'Hasan the potter, regain your senses
Hasan, cast a glance at your ruined house
How will the ovens of the children be filled?
O love-struck Hasan
Love is for the rich
Hasan, look around at your own hovel!'
To my ears, that sorrowful voice was akin

To someone calling a drowning man in a whirlpool
Those tears were light like flowers but
I, Hasan the potter, had been banished to that city of
    illusions
Where no sound, no movement
No shadow of a bird overhead
No sign of life remained!

Jahanzad, I am now in your street
In this cold darkness of the night
I stand again before your house
Hair tousled, mouth agape
From the window, those Caucasus-like magical eyes
Once again gaze at me
The world, Jahanzad, is a wheel where
Like goblets and glasses and vases, humans are built
    and broken
I am a human too
But these nine years I have spent in a funk of grief
Have turned Hasan the potter into a clod of earth
That does not harbour even a sign of moisture.

Jahanzad, in the market, at the shop of the old
    perfumer Yousuf
Your eyes have spoken to me again
And out of their beauty has emerged
A hint of moisture that may turn this clod of earth
    into clay again.

Who is aware of the limits of passion, Jahanzad, but
If you wish, I can again become that potter
Whose creations were the pride of palace and hovel
Of city and village

Which adorned the houses of rich and poor alike.
Who is aware of the limits of passion, Jahanzad, but
If you wish, I will return to my deserted pots
Those flowerpots filled with clay and nothingness
Toward the joy of creation and its display
That from that clay and nothingness, that colour and
       grease,
I produce again such sparks
That would light up the ruins of many a heart!

FAIZ

If there ever was a 'Mount Rushmore' of Urdu poetry, Faiz's face would be under serious contention for being carved in granite. Like Ghalib and Iqbal, Faiz Ahmed Faiz (1911–84) has been written about, translated and commented upon relentlessly. The official website of Faiz[1] contains audio files, and anyone looking to find a great collection of Faiz poems being sung, performed, declaimed and celebrated would do well to search for the poet's work on YouTube, and then proceed to knock themselves out in delight. Faiz's work has been well translated by V.G. Kiernan in a pleasing format that includes the poem in Urdu script, its transliteration and two forms of translation.[2]

Faiz was a Ghalibian, a Gandhian and a Marxist rolled into one. His poetry was infused with an unsurpassed lyricality, but spoke evocatively and urgently against regimes of exploitation. He was an early member of the Progressive Writers' Association, and formed a Punjab chapter in 1936. He wrote poems against colonialism, and after Independence/ Partition, settled in Lahore. He was among the Pakistanis who travelled to India in 1948 to attend Gandhi's funeral. His activism in the labour movement irked the right-wing elements in the Pakistani state, especially Ayub Khan. Months after Khan's elevation to the position of commander-in-chief of the Pakistan Army in 1951, Faiz and several of his colleagues were imprisoned under trumped-up conspiracy charges. He was incarcerated for four years, during which he wrote some of his finest poetry.[3] Even after his release, he was subject to surveillance and harassment, and spent a lot of years in quasi-exile in the Soviet Union and the Middle East where his poetry developed a truly international ethos. He won the Lenin Peace Prize in 1962, and things came full circle when the Government of Pakistan eventually awarded him its highest civilian honour, the Nishan-e Imtiaz (posthumously in 1990).

During his incarceration, Faiz's poetry exhibited a strong metaphorical connection with the trope of *qafas* (cage) and the relationship of the prisoner with the *saba* (breeze). His poems abounded with Sufi metaphors; for example, he incorporated Mansoor Hallaj's famous declaration '*An-al Haq*' ('I am God') as a political cry in his nazm '*Hum dekhenge*' ('We will see'; incidentally that particular nazm became the anthem of Pakistanis struggling for democratic rights and civil liberties under Zia-ul Haq; Iqbal Bano's magical rendition of the poem at the height of Zia's powers is a joy to hear).

In this volume, I have translated four of Faiz's poems, all of which have been extremely well performed by a number of well-known artistes.[4]

1   AAJ BAZAAR MEIN PAA-BAJAULAAN CHALO

> *Aaj bazaar mein paa-bajaulaan chalo*
> *Chashm-e nam, jaan-e shoreeda kaafi nahin*
> *Tohmat-e ishq-posheeda kaafi nahin*
> *Aaj bazaar mein paa-bajaulaan chalo*
>
> *Dast-afshan chalo, mast-o-raqsaan chalo*
> *Khaak bar-sar chalo, khoon ba-damaan chalo*

Raah takta hai sab shahr-e janaan chalo
Aaj bazaar mein paa-bajaulaan chalo

Haakim-e shahr bhi, majmaa-e aam bhi
Teer-e ilzaam bhi, sang-e dushnaam bhi
Subh-e nashaad bhi, roz-e nakaam bhi
Aaj bazaar mein paa-bajaulaan chalo

In ka dum-saaz apne siva kaun hai?
Shahr-e jaanan mein ab baa-safaa kaun hai?
Dast-e qaatil ke shaayaan raha kaun hai?
Rakht-e dil baandh lo, dil figaaro chalo
Phir hameen qatl ho aayen yaaro chalo.
Aaj bazaar mein paa-bajaulaan chalo.

COME IN SHACKLES TO THE MARKETPLACE

Come in shackles to the marketplace

The teary eye is not enough
Nor is the accusation of concealed love
Come in shackles to the marketplace

With hands held high, swaying and dancing, come
Walk with sand in your hair and blood on your
    shirtfront
The city of our beloved beckons, come
Come in shackles to the marketplace

The ruler of the city awaits, as does the multitude
The arrow of slander and the stone of invective awaits
    too

The forlorn morning too, and the unfulfilled day
Come in shackles to the marketplace

Who is their champion save us?
In the city of our beloved, is there anyone left pure?
Who is ready for the executioner's sword?
Pack up your hearts' belongings, O broken-hearted
    ones
Let it be us again who are murdered, friends

Come in shackles to the marketplace.

2   TUM AAYE HO NA SHAB-E INTEZAAR GUZRI HAI

Tum aaye ho na shab-e intezaar guzri hai
Talaash mein hai sahar, baar baar guzri hai

Junoon mein jitni bhi guzri, bakaar guzri hai
Agarche dil pe kharaabi hazaar guzri hai

Hui hai hazrat-e naaseh se guftagu jis shab
Vo shab zaroor sar-e ku-e yaar guzri hai

Vo baat saare fasaane mein jis ka zikr na tha
Vo baat un ko bahut na-gavaar guzri hai

Na gul khile hain, na unse mile, na mai pi hai
Ajeeb rang mein ab ke bahaar guzri hai

Chaman mein ghaarat-e gulcheen se jaane kya guzri
Qafas se aaj saba beqaraar guzri hai

NEITHER YOU CAME, NOR DID THIS NIGHT OF WAITING CEASE

Neither you came, nor did this night of waiting cease
The impatient morning has come and gone many times

The time spent in passion, was spent well
Even though the heart suffered its share of pain

Every night that the well-wisher advised me to desist
That night I spent at my lover's lane

That matter which was never mentioned in the story
Was the one to which my love took the greatest
offence

Neither roses bloomed, nor was my love met, nor
wine drunk
In such a strange way this spring has been squandered

I wonder what havoc the gardener wreaked on the
garden
For the zephyr has passed through my cage rather
agitated.[5]

3   SUBH-E AAZADI

Ye dagh dagh ujaala, ye shab-gazeeda sahar
Vo intezaar tha jis ka, ye vo sahar to nahin
Ye vo sahar to nahin jis ki aarzoo le kar
Chale thhe yaar, ke mil jaayegi kahin na kahin

Falak ke dasht mein taaron ki aakhri manzil
Kahin to hoga shab-e sust-mauj ka sahil
Kahin to jaa ke rukega safina-e gham-e dil

Jawaan lahu ki pur-asraar shah-raahon se
Chale jo yaar to daaman pe kitne haath pade
Dayaar-e husn ki be-sabr khwaab-gaahon se
Pukarti rahin baahen, badan bulaate rahe
Bahut azeez thi lekin rukh-e sahar ki lagan
Bahut qareen tha haseenaan-e noor ka daaman
Subuk subuk thi tamanna, dabi dabi thi thakan

Suna hai ho bhi chuka hai firaaq-e zulmat-o-noor
Suna hai ho bhi chuka hai visaal-e manzil-o-gaam
Badal chuka hai bahut ahl-e dard kaa dastoor
Nishaat-e vasl halaal aur azaab-e hijr haraam

Jigar ki aag, nazar ki umang, dil ki jalan
Kisi pe chaara-e hijran ka kuchh asar hi nahin
Kahaan se aayi nigaar-e saba, kidhar ko gayi?
Abhi chiragh-e sar-e rah ko kuchh khabar hi nahin

Abhi giraani-e shab mein kami nahin aayi
Najaat-e deeda-o-dil ki ghadi nahin aayi
Chale chalo, ke vo manzil abhi nahin aayi

THE DAWN OF FREEDOM

This pockmarked light, this night-inflected morning
This is not the dawn that we had awaited
Truly this is not the awaited dawn
That we friends had dreamed, sought, and in search set out.

The last harbour of the stars in the wasteland of the skies
Somewhere, there had to be a bank on this slow river
    of the night
Where the boat of the wounded heart could find ground
When we comrades walked on the tumultuous
    highways of young blood
So many hands clutched at our shirts to stall us
On the roads of beauty lay impatient boudoirs
Where embraces awaited, and bodies called out
But the face of the dawn was too beloved
The laps of the luminous beauties were too limited
And we went on, with bated passion, and muted
    exhaustion

And now they tell us that darkness and light have
    been separated
That journey and destination have finally been united
The experiences of the pain-afflicted are now
    transformed
Such that the joy of meeting is now legal and the pain
    of separation banned.

But is that true?
For the fire in my gut, the longing of my eyes, and the
    pain in my heart
Do not show any signs of being cured of parting
Where did the painted morn come from, where did it go?
The lamp at the highway has no news of it

The abatement of the darkness is not here yet
The deliverance awaited by eyes and hearts is not here
    yet
Keep moving, for the destination is not here yet.

4   MUJH SE PEHLI SI MOHABBAT, MERI MEHBOOB NA MAANG

Mujh se pehli si mohabbat, meri mehboob na maang

Main ne samjha thha ke tu hai to darakhshaan hai
        hayaat
Tera gham hai to gham-e dahr ka jhagda kya hai
Teri soorat se hai aalam mein bahaaron ko sabaat
Teri aankhon ke siva duniya mein rakhhaa kya hai
Tu jo mil jaaye to taqdeer nigoon ho jaaye
Yoon na thha, main ne faqat chaaha thhaa yoon ho jaaye

Aur bhi dukh hain zamaane mein mohabbat ke siva
Raahaten aur bhi hain vasl ki raahat ke siva

Anginat sadiyon ke taareek bahimaana tilism
Resham-o-atlas-o-kam-khwaab men bunvaaye huwe
Jaa-ba jaa bikte huwe koocha-o-bazaar mein jism
Khaak mein lithde huwe, khoon mein nahlaaye huwe
Jism nikle huwe amraaz ke tannooron se
Peep bahta hua gal-te huwe naasooron se
Laut jaati hai udhar ko bhi nazar, kya keeje?
Ab bhi dilkash hai tera husn magar kya keeje?
Aur bhi dukh hain zamaane mein mohabbat ke siva
Raahaten aur bhi hain vasl ki raahat ke siva

Mujh se pehli si mohabbat, meri mehboob na maang

MY LOVE, DO NOT ASK ME FOR THAT OLD LOVE AGAIN

My love, do not ask me for that old love again

I had felt that with you around, the world would be
    luminous

If I had your sorrows, what were the sorrows of this
    world worth?
Through your visage, spring had beauty
What else was left on this earth but your eyes?
If I could have you, my fortune would be resplendent
It was not to be, it was just my fantasy.

Indeed, there are more pains in the world than love
And more joys than the joy of union

For countless centuries, dark odious spells
Stand cloaked in silk and velvet and fine fabric
While on streets and markets, bodies are sold like
    commodities
Coated with dust, bathed in blood
Bodies fresh out of the ovens of disease
Pus flowing quietly from rotting, unhealed wounds
But the gaze returns there too, what am I to do?
Your beauty is alluring still, but what am I to do?

Indeed, there are more pains in the world than love
And more joys than the joy of union

My love, do not ask me for that old love again.

MIRAJI

Sanaullah Dar 'Miraji' (1912–49) burnt the candle of his life at both ends, and died tragically young, but not before he produced a corpus of poetry that has stood the test of time. As a title, he took on the name of a woman he was infatuated with. This act may be seen, in hindsight, as his attempt to decentre the patriarchy and heteronormativity that afflicted Urdu poetry in the twentieth century.[1] His poetry traversed the spectrum, from relatively simple ghazals and nazms to complex surreal tracts. The influence of Charles Baudelaire on Miraji was profound, but he was also struck by the lyricality of Omar Khayyam, whom he translated into Urdu.

Miraji briefly headed the Halqa-e Arbaab-e Zauq (circle of connoisseurs), a literary organization that was formed in 1939, and infused Urdu poetry with modernism. He was himself a modern character, who affected a bohemian appearance and liberated much of his verse from the prison of rhyme and metre, while still tossing out the occasional classical ghazal. The one I have translated below was immortalized by Ghulam Ali. I have also included a nazm that is more reflective of his oeuvre.

1   BHOOL GAYA

Nagri nagri phira musafir ghar ka rasta bhool gaya
Kya hai tera kya hai mera apna paraaya bhool gaya

164

Apni beeti jag beeti hai, jab se dil ne jaan liya
Hanste hanste jeevan beeta, rona dhona bhool gaya

Andhiyaare se ek kiran ne jhaank ke dekha,
sharmaayi
Dhund si chhab to yaad rahi, kaisa thha chehra bhool gaya

Hansi hansi mein, khel khel mein baat ki baat mein
rang gaya
Dil bhi hote hote aakhir ghaao ka risna bhool gaya

Ek nazar ki, ek hi pal ki baat hai dori saanson ki
Ek nazar ka noor mitaa, jab ek pal beeta bhool gaya

Jis ko dekho us ke dil mein shikvaa hai to itna hai
Hamen to sab kuchh yaad raha, par ham ko zamaana
bhool gaya

Koi kahe ye kis ne kaha thha, keh do jo kuchh ji mein hai
'Miraji' keh kar pachhtaayaa, aur phir kehna bhool gaya

HE FORGOT

The wayfarer went from town to town, the way back, he
forgot
His possessions, his friends and foes, he lost track, he
forgot

Once the heart knew that the experience of self and
world were one
It started laughing so hard, to let sobs wrack, it forgot

A lone sunbeam broke through the dark, it looked
    and shyly smiled
Made out a face, but its features in the dark it forgot

In playful laughing talk with you, I became
    enamoured
Although my heart remained wounded, your attack it
    forgot

Each glance and each moment is part of life's evolving
    string
A glance lost its radiant light, when a moment one
    forgot

Whoever I meet has one major complaint with the
    world
'I remembered everyone's woes, my woes the world
    forgot'

I don't remember who urged me to bravely say my
    piece
'Miraji,' I said with regret, and to say more, forgot.

2   **SAFAR**

Tum ne tahreek mujhe di ke jaao dekho
Chaand taaron se pare aur duniyaayein hain
Tum ne hi mujh se kaha tha ki khabar le aao
Mere dil mein vahin jaane ki tamanaayen hain

Aur main chal diya ghaur kiya kab is par
Kitna mehdood hai insaan ki quvvat ka tilism

Bas yahi ji ko khayaal aaya, tumhen khush kar doon
Ye na socha ke yoon mit jaayega raahat ka tilism

Aur ab humdami-o-ishrat-e raftaa kaise
Aah! Ab doori hai, doori hai, faqat doori hai
Tum kahin aur main kahin, ab nahin pehli haalat
Laut ke aa bhi nahin saktaa ye hai majboori

Meri qismat ke judaai tumhen manzoor hui
Meri qismat ko pasand aayi na meri baaten
Ab nahin jalvaagah-e khilavat-e shab afsaane
Ab to bas teeraa-o-taareek hai apni raaten.

JOURNEY

You commanded me, go on and see
There are worlds beyond the moon and stars
And it was you who bade me get news
For your heart desired to visit those worlds as well.

And I headed off, without realizing, reflecting
How limited the power of humanity is, its spell
I just desired that you should be happy, did not know
That the spell that would break would be of my
    contentment.

And now, where is the companionship, the desire for
    the past?
Ah, all that is left is distance. And distance. Only distance.
You are somewhere, I elsewhere; the earlier situation
    was not to be
And this is a journey where return is impossible.

It is my fate that separation was acceptable to you
But my fate did not like my words
No more the privacy of the evening tales
My nights are now nothing, just dark and opaque.

ALI SARDAR JAFRI

For some reason, Ali Sardar Jafri (1913–2000) never received his due as a poet, perhaps due to his programmatic verses and his overt association with the Communist Party of India. In his later years, he experienced some recognition as a poet who wrote optimistically about Indo-Pakistan relations. When Indian Prime Minister Atal Bihari Vajpayee took a bus journey to Pakistan in 1999, the following four-liner by Jafri was played on its PA system, and became quite the rage for a while:

Tum aao gulshan-e Lahore se chaman bardosh
Hum aayen subh-e Banaras ki raushni le kar
Himalaya ki havaaon ki taazgi le kar
Aur us ke baad yeh poochhenge kaun dushman hai?

Come bearing the fragrant garden of Lahore
And we will bring the light of a Banaras morning
And the fresh breeze from the Himalayas
And then let us ask: who is the enemy?

Jafri began his career as a fiction writer, but later moved to poetry. He also wrote a few plays for the Indian People's Theatre Association. He was subjected to periodic incarceration twice: first, by the British in 1939, and then—in a moment that reminds us of Frantz Fanon's account of the betrayal of the moment of decolonization by local elites—Jafri was arrested by the government of independent India in 1949 for espousing the cause of socialism, joining his colleagues like Faiz and Sajjad Zaheer who had suffered similar incarceration in Pakistan. Like a good communist, he also aroused the ire of religious fundamentalists, and was subjected to death threats in the 1980s when he came out against the treatment of divorced women under the Muslim Personal Law. His opposition to the infamous Muslim Women's Protection Act in 1986 earned him the ire of Muslim communalists; I remember, as a college student, watching him being shouted at, slapped and garlanded with chappals by goons—a moment that politicized me further against the atmosphere of rapidly increasing communalism in India. However, in the end, we must remember that Jafri led a celebrated life, having had the Jnanpith award bestowed on him in 1993. In 2013, on the occasion of his birth centenary, a website was inaugurated in his honour.[1]

Jafri's long poem '*Karbala*'—recited by him—is available in the public domain, and has been translated by my friend Syed Akbar Hyder in his book *Reliving Karbala*.[2] I have chosen to translate two other poems here. The first is his '*Guftagu Band Na Ho*', speaking of the possibilities of more harmonious Indo-Pakistan relations. The second is an excerpt from Jafri's long poem '*Avadh ki Khaak-e Haseen*' ('The Beautiful Land of Avadh'). I include the latter as an exemplar of progressive poetry, which turned labour into romance and ordinary folk into protagonists.

1   GUFTAGU BAND NA HO

Guftagu band na ho
Baat se baat chale
Subh tak shaam-e mulaaqaat chale
Hum pe hansti hui ye taaron bhari raat chale

Vo jo alfaaz ke haathon mein hai sang-e dushnaam
Tanz chhalkaye to chhalkaaya karen zahr ke jaam
Teekhi nazren hon tarash abru-e khamdaar rahe
Ban pade jaise bhi dil seenon mein, bedaar rahe
Bebasi harf ko zanjeer ba-paa kar na sake
Koi qaatil ho magar qatl-e nava kar na sake

Subh tak dhal ke koi harf-e vafaa aayega
Ishq aayegaa ba-sad laghzish-e paa aayega
Nazren jhuk jaayengi, dil dhadkenge, lab kaanpengey
Khamoshi bosa-e lab ban ke bahak jayegi
Sirf ghunchon ke chatakne ki sadaa aayegi

Aur phir harf-o-nava ki na zaroorat hogi
Chashm-o-abroo ke ishaaron mein mohabbat hogi
Nafrat uth jaayegi, mehmaan muravvat hogi

Haath mein haath liye, saara jahaan saath liye
Tohfa-e dard liye, pyaar ki saughaat liye
Regzaaron se adaawat ke guzar jaayeingey
Khoon ke daryaaon se hum paar utar jaayeingey

Guftagu band na ho
Baat se baat chale
Subh tak shaam-e mulaaqaat chale
Hum pe hansti hui ye taaron bhari raat chale

LET NOT THE CONVERSATION CEASE

Let not the conversation cease
Let one word lead to another
And let our evening tryst go on till dawn
While the starry night-sky smiles down on us

Though we have hurled the stones of bitter words at
       each other
We have swirled poison in our goblets in the form of
       sarcastic jibes
Our brows furrowed, our gazes venomous
But be that as it may, let hearts awaken in chests
Let not despair imprison our words
Whoever the murderers are, let them not kill dialogue

If that is done, a word of faith may escape at dawn
Love will arrive on trembling legs
Eyes downcast, hearts aflutter, lips atremble
Silence will then be fragrant like a kiss on the lips
And the only sound left will be that of buds flowering

And then there will be need for neither word nor talk
In the movement of the gaze, an emotion will sprout
Tenderness will be our guest, hate will be asked to leave

Hand in hand, accompanied by the whole world
Bearing the gift of pain, and the bounty of fondness
We will cross the deserts of animus
And find ourselves on the other side of oceans of blood

Let not the conversation cease
Let one word lead to another
And let our evening tryst go on till dawn
While the starry night-sky smiles down on us.

2   AVADH KI KHAAK-E HASEEN[3]

Ye seedhe saadhe ghareeb insan, nekiyon ke
       mujassame hain
Ye mehnaton ke khuda, ye takhleekh ke payambar

Jo apne haathon ke khurdarepan se zindagi ko
    sanvaarte hain
Lohaar ke ghan ke neeche lohe hi shakl tabdeel ho
    rahi hai
Kumhaar ka chaak chal raha hai
Suraahiyan raqs kar rahi hain
Safed aata siyaah chakki se raag ban kar nikal raha hai
Sunehre choolhon mein aag ke phool khil rahe hain
Pateeliyaan gunguna rahi hain
Dhuen se kaale tave bhi chingaariyon ke honton se
    hans rahe hain
Dupatte aangan mein doriyon se tange hue hain
Aur un ke aanchal se dhaani boonden tapak rahi hain
Sunehri pagdandiyon ke dil par
Siyaah lehngon ki surkh koten chamak rahi hain
Ye saadgi kis qadar haseen hai
Main jail mein baithe baithe aksar ye sochta hoon
Jo ho sake to Avadh ki pyaari zameen ko god mein
    utha loon
Aur us ke shadaab lahlahaati jabeen ko
Hazaaron boson se jagmaga doon.

THE BEAUTIFUL LAND OF AVADH

These simple poor folk are the epitome of goodness
These gods of labour, these prophets of creation
Who make life beautiful with their calloused hands
Under the blacksmith's anvil, iron is changing shape
The potter's wheel hums
And goblets dance to its beat
The white flour emerges from the black millstone like
    a musical note

Flowers of fire bloom in stoves and ovens
Cooking utensils sing along
Skillets black with smoke laugh with lips made of
  sparks
Dupattas hang on ropes
And from their borders, a row of drops fall to the
  ground
On the hearts of these golden streets
The red borders of black long skirts shine on
How beautiful is this simplicity!
I sit in my prison cell and often wonder
That if I could I would take the beautiful earth of my
  Avadh in my lap
And light up its beautiful, shimmering forehead
With thousands of kisses.

JAN NISAR AKHTAR

Bhoole na kisi haal mein aadaab-e nazar hum
Mud kar na tujhe dekh sake waqt-e safar hum
Jeene ka hamen khud na mila waqt to kya hai
Auron ko sikhlaate rahe jeene ka hunar hum

I never did lose sight of the protocols of the gaze
Thus did not turn to say goodbye as we went our ways
I admit I had no time to lead my own life but
My advice guided so many through its tricky maze.

A little birdie persistently whispers that Jan Nisar Akhtar (1914–76) ghostwrote many of the film songs that Sahir got credit for. Such rumours are not particularly useful, since they cannot be confirmed, but they do serve as a reminder that Jan Nisar's style was similar to Sahir's, and his command over poetry was as strong.[1] Akhtar himself is credited with quite a few song lyrics, such as the haunting '*Ye dil aur un ki nigahon ke saaye*' ('This heart, and the shadow of the gaze') from the 1973 film *Prem Parbat*, and '*Ai dil-e nadaan*' ('O naive heart') from the 1983 film *Razia Sultan*.

Jan Nisar gave up a career as an academic and moved to Bombay, where he mostly hung out with Mulk Raj Anand, Krishan Chander, Rajinder Singh Bedi and Ismat Chughtai—the so-called 'Bombay Group of Writers'. He published several anthologies of his work, including *Khaak-e Dil* (The Dust of the Heart; 1973).

I have translated two of his poems. The first, 'Ash-aar Mere' ('My Verses'), was rendered beautifully by Mukesh in a non-film work.[2] The second poem hews more to the progressive tradition. 'Aakhri Lamha' ('Last Moment') is part of a long poem dedicated to his daughter Uneza. The poem incorporates narrative sweeps, shifting rhyme schemes and combines personal narrative with broader social concerns.

1 ASH-AAR MERE

Ash-aar mere yoon to zamaane ke liye hain
Kuchh sher faqat unko sunaane ke liye hain

Ab ye bhi nahin theek ki har dard mitaa den
Kuchh dard kaleje se lagaane ke liye hain

Aankhon mein jo bhar loge to kaanton se chubhenge
Ye khwaab to palkon pe sajaane ke liye hain

Dekhoon tere haathon ko to lagta hai tere hath
Mandir mein faqat deep jalaane ke liye hain

Socho to badi cheez hai tahzeeb badan ki
Varna to badan aag bujhaane ke liye hain

Ye ilm ka sauda, ye risaale ye kitaaben
Ek shakhs ki yaadon ko bhulaane ke liye hain

MY VERSES

My poetry of course for the entire world I deploy
But some verses are set aside for that one person's joy

Some deep wounds are meant to be kept in the heart
    closely guarded
No joy can compensate if those unique pains are
    destroyed

Store them not inside your eyes, they will sting you
    like sharp thorns
Place those sharp shards of dreams on your eyelashes,
    to enjoy

When I look at your wondrous hands, I do strongly
    believe
To light lamps in temples, they are destined to be
    employed

Considered one way, the discipline of the flesh is vital
Think differently, and the body's merely a pleasure-toy

This lofty intellectual demeanour I affect, sir
Is but a vain attempt to forget someone—a mere ploy.

2   **AAKHRI LAMHA**

(APNI BETI UNEZA KE NAAM)[3]

Tum meri zindagi mein aayi ho
Mera ek paaon jab rikaab mein hai
Dil ki dhadkan hai doobne ke qareeb
Saans har lahza pech-o-taab mein hai
Toot-te bekharosh taaron ki
Aakhri kapkai rabab mein ha
Koi manzil, na jaada-e manzil
Raasta gum kisi saraab mein hai

Tum ko chaaha kiya khayaalon mein
Tum ko paaya bhi jaise khwaab mein hai

Main sochta thha ke tum aaogi, tumhe paakar
Main is jahaan ke dukh-o-dard bhool jaaoonga
Gale mein daal ke baanhen jo jhool jaaogi
Main aasmaan ke tare bhi tod laaoonga

Tum ek bel ke manind badhti jaaogi
Na chhoo sakengi havaadis ki aandhiyan tum ko
Main apni jaan pe sau aafaten utha loonga
Chhupa ke rakkhoonga baahon ke darmiyan tum ko

Magar main aaj bahut door jaane vaala hoon
Bas aur chand nafas ko tumhare paas hoon main
Tumhe jo paa ke khushi hai, tum is khushi pe na jaao
Tumhe ye ilm nahin kis qadar udaas hoon main

Kya tum ko khabar is duniya ki, kya tum ko pataa is
        duniya ka
Masoom dilon ko dukh dena, ik sheva hai is duniya ka
Taareeq bataayegi tum ko insaan se kahaan par bhool hui
Sarmaaye ke haathon duniya ki kis tarah mohabbat
        dhool hui
Jeene ki hara tarah se tamanna haseen hai
Har shar ke bavajood ye duniya haseen hai
Dariya ki tund bhaad bhayaanak sahi magar
Toofan se khelta hua tinka haseen hai
Sehra ka har sukoot daraata rahe to kya
Jangal ko kaat-ta hua rasta haseen hai

Chaman se chand hi kaante main chun saka lekin
Badi hai baat jo tum rang-e gul nikhaar sako

Amal tumhara ye taufeeq de sake tum ko
Ke zindagi ka har ek qarz tum utaar sako

Raushni der se aankhon ki bujhi jaati hai
Theek se kuchh bhi dikhai nahin deta mujh ko
Ek chehra mere chehre pe jhuka jaata hai
Kaun hai ye bhi sujhayi nahin deta mujh ko
Sirf sannate ki awaaz chali aati hai
Aur to kuchh bhi sunaai nahin deta mujh ko

Ye meri nazm mera pyaar hai tumhaare liye
Ye sher tum ko meri rooh ka pata denge
Yehi tumhe mere azm-o-amal ki denge khabar
Yehi tumhe meri majbooriyan bataayenge
Kabhi jo gham ke andhere mein dagmagaaogi
Tumhari raah mein kitne diye jalaayenge

Aao is chaand se maathe ko zara choom to loon
Phir na hoga hamen ye pyaar naseeb aa jaao
Aaakhri lamha hai seene pe mere sar rakh do
Dil ki haalat hui jaati hai ajeeb aa jaao
Na aizza na akhibba na khuda hai na rasool
Koi is waqt nahin mere qareeb, aa jaao
Tum to qareeb aa jaao

THE LAST MOMENT
(FOR MY DAUGHTER UNEZA)

You have come into my life now
When departing, I have one foot on the stirrup
When my heartbeat has begun to get faint
And every breath is a tortured effort

A final sound escapes, as if
From the frayed strings of a harp
Neither a destination, nor a pathway to one
My path is ghostly, like a mirage
I had desired you in my thoughts
And now have found you as if in a dream

I had thought that when you came, your presence
Would help me forget all the woes of this world
That when you swung in my joyous embrace
I would bring you back the stars from the sky

You would grow tall like a sturdy vine
The storms of circumstance would not reach you
A hundred calamities I would take upon myself
Keeping you safely nestled in my arms

But today, I am headed to a place far away
I am your companion for a few short moments
Do not go by the happiness I feel in your presence
You have no idea how sad I am

What do you know of this world, what do you reckon
    of this world?
To torture innocent hearts is a pastime of this world
History will show us where humanity lost its way
How love was ground to dust by the merciless hand
    of capital

Every will to live is beautiful
Despite all its flaws, the world is beautiful
The storm of a river in spate is scary, but
That stubborn floater in the maelstrom is beautiful

The stillness of the desert does terrify, so what?
The path that cuts through the forest is beautiful

I was able to remove very few thorns from the garden, but
It would be great if you could bring colour back to
      the roses
May your effort give you the wisdom
That you may repay every debt that you owe to life

The light in my eyes has begun to dim
I can no longer see anything with clarity
A face bends over mine
But whose is it? I can no longer tell
The only sound is the sound of silence
I can hear nothing else

This poem is an offering of my love
These verses will show you the way to my soul
It is they who will tell you of my struggle, my effort
It is they who will show you my constraints
When you will reel in the darkness of sorrows
It is they who will light so many lamps in your path

Come, that I may kiss that bright moonlike forehead
We may never be destined for such love, come
It is the final moment: rest your head on my chest
My heart has begun to experience strange feelings, come
No friends, no relatives, no God, no prophets
There is no one near me, come
At least you be close, come.

MAJROOH SULTANPURI

Majrooh, likh rahe hain vo ahl-e vafaa ke naam
Hum bhi khade hue hain gunahgaar ki tarah

Majrooh, the names of the faithful they write
Like a sinner, I await my name, quiet

Asrar-ul Hassan Khan 'Majrooh' (1919–2000) was born in Sultanpur, and studied in relatively conventional settings, becoming a qualified *Unani* hakim, a career he gave up to become a full-time poet. His high-risk career choice was to pay rich dividends; he became arguably the most successful poet of the progressive tradition after Sahir, writing extensively for movies.

Majrooh's leftist leanings were evident from the start, as was his lyricality. He combined both by writing exquisite ghazals in praise of socialist nations (the maqta of one of his ghazals was: '*Meri nigaah mein hai arz-e Moscow, Majrooh / Vo sarzameen ke sitaare jise salaam karen*'; 'My eyes are fixed on the horizon of Moscow, Majrooh / The land that is saluted even by the stars'). Despite his activism during the independence movement, Majrooh escaped incarceration in the pre-1947 phase. Ironically, he was jailed in 1949 (along with fellow lefty film-wala Balraj Sahni and fellow PWA member Ali Sardar Jafri, among others) by the government of newly independent India, which reflected the troubling reality of how newly independent nations devoured their socialists after decolonization.

The ghazal I have translated below is a tongue-in-cheek look at how lovers and revolutionaries bragged about their misfortune to mark their superiority.[1] To do justice to Majrooh's phenomenal success as a lyricist (he is, after all, the only lyricist to have won the prestigious Dadasaheb Phalke Award), I also include a film song. His most popular songs were '*Chahoonga main tujhe saanjh savere*' (from the 1946 *Dosti*), the execrable '*Angrezi mein kehte hain ke I love you*' (from the 1982 film *Khuddar*) and '*Papa kehte hain bada naam karega*' (from the 1988 film *Qayamat se Qayamat Tak*). I would, in good cricketing tradition, do a 'well-left' to all three. I have chosen the song '*Ek din bik jaayega maati ke mol*' from the 1975 film *Dharam Karam*, especially since it truly showcases Majrooh's lyrical ability, and simultaneously demonstrates how a song is different from a traditional poem.

1 TUM SE ZIYAADA

> *Hum ko junoon kya sikhlaate ho, hum thhe pareshan
>   tum se ziyaada*
> *Chaak kiye hain hum ne azeezo, chaar garebaan tum
>   se ziyaada*
>
> *Chaak-e jigar muhtaaj-e rafoo hai, aaj to daaman sirf
>   lahoo hai*
> *Ek mausam thha, hum ko raha hai shauq-e bahaaran
>   tum se ziyaada*
>
> *Ahd-e vafaa yaaron se nibhaayen, naaz-e hareefan
>   hans ke uthaayen*

Jab hamein armaan tum se siva thha, ab hai
    pashemaan tum se ziyaada

Jao tum apni baam ki khaatir saari laven sham'on ki
    katar lo
Zakhmon ke mehr-o-maah salaamat, jashn-e
    chiraaghan tum se ziyaada

Hum bhi hamesha qatl hue, aur tum ne bhi dekha
    door se, lekin
Ye na samajhna hum ko hua hai jaan ka nukhsan tum
    se ziyaada

Zanjeer-o-deevaar hi dekhi tum ne to, Majrooh,
    magar hum
Koocha koocha dekh rahe hain aalam-e zindaan tum
    se ziyaada

WAY MORE THAN YOU

Do not teach me about passion, I've suffered hurt way
    more than you
I have torn in lost love, my friend, four more good
    shirts, way more than you

Wounded hearts demand repairing, my garment is red
    with my blood
Once there was a blighted autumn, when I sought
    spring way more than you

Faithful was I to well-wishers, and smilingly bore the
    betrayal of foes

More than you I was passionate; now I'm shamefaced
    way more than you

Hide behind your darkened secrets, cut the wicks off
    prying tapers
Yet, my wounds will light up the night: illumination
    way more than you

Though I was always killed in action, and you always
    watched from safety
Do not imagine that I suffered annihilation way more
    than you[2]

Walls and chains were all you knew, but know this,
    Majrooh, even then
Every street is like a prison: incarceration way more
    than you.

2   EK DIN BIK JAYEGA

Ek din bik jayega, maati ke mol
Jag mein reh jayenge pyare tere bol
Dooje ke honthon ko de kar apne geet
Koi nishani chhod, phir duniya se dol

Anhoni path mein kaante lakh bichhaaye
Honi to phir bhi bichhda yaar milaye
Ye birha, ye doori
Do pal ki majboori
Phir koi dilwala kahe ko ghabraye
Taram pam . . .
Dhara jo behti hai milke rehti hai
Behti dhara ban ja, phir duniya se dol

Ek din bik jayega, maati ke mol
Jag mein reh jayenge pyare tere bol

Parde ke peechhe baithi saanval gori
Thaam ke tere mere man ki dori
Ye dori na chhoote, ye bandhan na toote
Bhor hone wali hai ab raina hai thodi
Taram pam . . .
Sar ko jhukaye tu baitha kya hai yaar?
Gori se naina jod, phir duniya se dol

Ek din bik jayega, maati ke mol
Jag mein reh jayenge pyare tere bol

YOU WILL BE SOLD ONE DAY

A day will come when you will be sold for the price
    of dust
Remember, all that will be left will be your poems, just
Donate your songs to strangers' lips and they'll keep
    you alive
Leave this eternal gift for them, and then move on
    you must.

Chance will strew a million thorns on your path till
    the end
While fortune will unite you with old forgotten friends
This autumn, this parting
A brief pain, a smarting
Why should the brave of heart be scared of fortune then?
Taram pum . . .

Watch when the river flows: many eddies, one thrust
Become the flowing stream, and then move on you must

A day will come when you will be sold for the price
      of dust
Remember, all that will be left will be your poems, just

Look, behind the curtain sits a brown beauty divine
She holds in her hands a string, controls your mind
      and mine
Let not that string break; let not that relationship fade
For it will soon be morning, and a harsh light will
      invade
Taram pum . . .
Don't sit, bowing your head, my young friend robust
Lock eyes with that beauty, and then move on you
      must

A day will come when you will be sold for the price
      of dust
Remember, all that will be left will be your poems, just.

KAIFI AZMI

Hua hai hukm ke Kaifi ko sang-saar karo
Maseeh baithe hain chhup kar kahaan, khuda jaane

Stone Kaifi to death, the rulers cried
The Messiah? We do not know where he hides!

Born Syed Athar Hussain Rizvi (1919–2002), Kaifi Azmi was initially educated in Islamic seminaries, but eventually became a true adherent of Marxism, dedicating his life to the service of the Communist Party of India, and writing his most tortured work, *Aavara Sajde* (Vagabond Obeisances), when the CPI and CPM split in the 1960s. He is well known for his proclamation: 'I was born in enslaved India, have lived in independent secular India, and God willing, I will die in socialist India.' Alas, his last wish was not to come true; indeed, the year he died was especially difficult even for secular India, thanks to the Gujarat pogroms. Kaifi's death became a moment when people took it upon themselves to rededicate themselves to the idea of secularism.

Kaifi won many awards in his life, but was proudest of his Soviet Land Nehru Award. The Urdu Academy conferred on him the Millennium Award in 2001, and he was awarded the Sahitya Akademi Fellowship in 2002. His presence is well represented on the web[1], and translations[2] of his work have been well received.

I have translated two poems below. The first, 'Andeshe' ('Premonitions') is a poignant description of an ending relationship, and was adapted by Chetan Anand in the 1964 film *Haqeeqat*, picturized on soldiers presumed dead in the Indo-China war imagining their spouses grieving them. In the second poem 'Makaan' ('House'), Kaifi writes about construction workers and their role in the conquest of nature. In its unselfconscious modernism, the poem extols the power of labour in achieving mastery over nature (through the use of walls, and cables of electricity), and is reminiscent of a similar poem by Majaz on the train, also translated in this volume, albeit with a lot more anger on behalf of the dispossessed workers. To me, the poem depicts the ultimate potential failure of modernity from the point of view of the socialist: that it does not automatically ensure a just and egalitarian society. Modernity sometimes fails the very subjects who were promised freedom from the feudal system they had laboured under in earlier eras. Kaifi ends with a call for collective action, which is a trope he was to deploy consistently in his work.

1   ANDESHE

> *Rooh bechain hai, ek dil ki aziyyat kya hai*
> *Dil hi shola hai to ye soz-e mohabbat kya hai*
> *Vo mujhe bhool gayi iski shikaayat kya hai*
> *Ranj to ye hai ke ro-ro ke bhulaayaa hoga*
>
> *Jhuk gayi hogi javaan-saal umangon ki jabeen*
> *Mit gayi hogi lalak, doob gaya hoga yaqeen*
> *Chha gaya hoga dhuaan ghoom gayi hogi zameen*
> *Apne pehle hi gharaonde ko jo dhaayaa hoga*

Dil ne aise bhi kuchh afsaane sunaaye honge
Ashk aankhon ne piye aur na bahaaye honge
Band kamre mein jo khat mere jalaaye honge
Ek-ik harf jabeen par ubhar aaya hoga

Us ne ghabra ke nazar lakh bachayi hogi
Mit ke ik naqsh ne sau shakl dikhaayi hogi
Mez se jab meri tasveer hataayi hogi
Har taraf mujh ko tadapta hua paaya hoga

Bemahal chhed pe jazbaat ubal aaye honge
Gham pashemaan tabassum mein dhal aaye honge
Naam par mere jab aansoo nikal aaye honge
Sar na kaandhe se saheli ke uthaaya hoga

Zulf zid kar ke kisi ne jo banayi hogi
Roothe jalvon pe khizaan aur bhi chhayi hogi
Barq ashvon ne kayi din na girayi hogi
Rang chehre pe kayi roz na aaya hoga

PREMONITIONS

The soul itself is upset; it's not merely the heart's pain
The heart is all afire, agony is a refrain
I'm not sad that she forgot me and scrubbed
    memory's stain
But she did it with tears and hurt—that is what I regret.

Resigned, her young expectations must have bowed
    their forehead
Her certitude must have sunk to resignation with dread

A pall of smoke might have set in, the earth turned on
    its head
When her first dream-nest she was forced to destroy
    and forget.

The heart must have narrated to her such a complex
    tale
That she would have held back her tears composed
    and calm, but pale
But when she burned my letters in a closed room with
    a wail
Every word must have floated up and made her eyes
    more wet.

Scared, she must have avoided each recriminating
    gaze
But in a hundred images, she may have seen my face
When she must have moved my picture from its
    familiar place
She would have found me everywhere, a painful
    silhouette.

An innocent tease may have led emotions to overflow
Her tentative and bashful smiles would have betrayed
    sorrow
But when she burst into tears at my name, don't I know
Her head on her friend's shoulder would have stayed,
    upset.

If friends insisted on making her up, combing her hair,
Her saddened beauty must have seemed so barren and
    bare

Her face would strike no lightning awhile in hearts
    debonair
It would not have regained colour for days, alas not yet.

2   **MAKAAN**

Aaj ki raat bahut garm hawaa chalti hai
Aaj ki raat na footpath pe neend aayegi
Sab utho, main bhi uthoon, tum bhi utho, tum bhi utho
Koi khidki isi deewaar mein khul jaayegi

Ye zameen tab bhi nigal lene pe aamaada thhi
Paaon jab toot'ti shaakhon se utaare hum ne,
Un makaanon ko khabar hai, na makeenon ko khabar
Un dinon ki jo gufaaon mein guzaare hum ne
Haath dhalte gaye saanchon mein to thakte kaise
Naqsh ke baad naye naqsh nikhaare hum ne
Ki ye deewaar buland, aur buland, aur buland
Baam-o-dar aur, zaraa aur sanwaare hum ne
Aandhiyaan tod liya karti thhi shamon ki laven
Jad diye is liye bijli ke sitaare hum ne

Ban gaya qasr, to pehre pe koi baith gaya
So rahe khaak pe hum shorish-e taameer liye
Apni nas nas mein liye mehnat-e paiham ki thhakan
Band aankhon mein usi qasr ki tasveer liye
Din pighalta hai usi tarha saron par ab bhi
Raat aankhon mein khatakti hai siyah teer liye
Aaj ki raat bahut garm hawaa chalti hai
Aaj ki raat na footpath pe neend aayegi
Sab utho, main bhi uthoon, tum bhi utho, tum bhi utho
Koi khidki isi deewaar mein khul jaayegi

HOUSE

A hot air blows tonight
It will be impossible to sleep on the pavement
Arise everyone! I will rise too. And you. And yourself
    too
That a window may open in these very walls.

The earth had forever threatened to swallow us
Since we descended from trees and became human,
Neither these houses, nor their residents care to remember
All those days humanity spent in caves.
Once our arms learned the craft however, how could
    they tire?
Design after design took shape through our work.
And then we built the walls higher, higher and yet higher
Lovingly wrought an even greater beauty to the
    ceilings and doors
Storms used to extinguish the flames of our lamps
So we fixed stars made of electricity in our skies.

Once the palace was built, they hired a guard to keep
    us out
And we slept in the dirt, with our screaming craft
Our pulses pounding with exhaustion
Bearing the picture of that very palace in our tightly
    shut eyes
The day still melts on our heads like before
The night pierces our eyes with black arrows,
A hot air blows tonight
It will be impossible to sleep on the pavement
Arise everyone! I will rise too. And you. And yourself too
That a window may open in these very walls.

SAHIR LUDHIANVI

Before he was Sahir Ludhianvi[1], Abdul Hai (1921–80) was born in a family of Punjabi landowners. His anger at his class position led to his expulsion from college. However, even before he turned twenty-five, he had published *Talkhiyan*, a bestseller till date. Sahir, of course, is known in the public imagination for his incredible career as a film lyricist. A partial collection of his film lyrics titled *Gaata Jaaye Banjara* (And the Gypsy Sings On) outsells most poetry books in serious bookstores. Sahir has been credited with recasting class-rebellion as romantic rebellion in film songs to shoehorn his politics into the filmi idiom. However, he was strangely ignored by the intelligentsia. For example, in his analysis of Urdu literature Mohammed Sadiq, after a chapter each on Ghalib, Iqbal, and even Akbar Allahabadi, dismisses Sahir in one paragraph. His analysis begins thus: 'Though deficient in imagination, Sahir has a strong intellectual approach.'[2]

But despite being ignored by some of the intelligentsia, the poet lives on in the public imagination. In this crowded field, let me declare that despite all his flaws, Sahir is my favourite poet, and his *Parchhaiyan* my favourite poem. It has to do with a variety of personal reasons, and I will not be aghast if this surprises some readers.

I have chosen to translate three poems from Sahir here. The first is his uber-famous '*Taj Mahal*', which was sung beautifully by Mohammad Rafi in the 1964 film *Ghazal*. The second is a qataa that exemplifies the defiance of Sahir the poet. The third is a selection from his film work: '*Main pal do pal ka shaayar hoon*' from the blockbuster 1976 film *Kabhie Kabhie*.

1   TAJ MAHAL

> *Taj tere liye ek mazhar-e ulfat hi sahi*
> *Tujh ko is vaadi-e rangeen se aqeedat hi sahi*
> *Meri mehboob, kahin aur mila kar mujh se!*
>
> *Bazm-e shahi mein ghareebon ka guzar kya maani?*
> *Sabt jis rah pe hon satvat-e shaahi ke nishan*
> *Us pe ulfat bhari roohon ka safar kya maani?*
>
> *Meri mehboob, pas-e parda-e tashheer-e vafaa*
> *Tu ne satvat ke nishaanon ko to dekha hota?*
> *Murda shahon ke maqaabir se bahalne vaali*
> *Apne taareek makaanon ko to dekha hota?*
>
> *Anginat logon ne duniya mein mohabbat ki hai*
> *Kaun kehta hai ke sadeq na thhe jazbe un ke?*
> *Lekin un ke liye tash-heer ka saamaan nahin*
> *Kyon ke vo log bhi apni hi tarah muflis thhe*
>
> *Ye imaaraat, vo maqaabir, ye faseelen, ye hisaar*
> *Mutlaq-ul hukm shahenshahon ki azmat ke sutoon*
> *Daaman-e dahr pe us rang ki gulkaari hai*
> *Jis mein shaamil hai tere aur mere ajdaad ka khoon*
>
> *Meri mehboob, unhen bhi to mohabbat hogi*
> *Jin ki sannaai ne bakhshi hai isey shakl-e jameel*

Un ke pyaaron ke maqaabir rahe benaam-o-namood
Aaj tak un pe jalaayi na kisi ne qandeel

Ye chamanzaar, ye Jamunaa ka kinaaraa, ye mahal
Ye munaqqash dar-o-deevaar, ye mehraab, ye taaq
Ek shahenshah ne daulat ka sahara le kar
Ham ghareebon ki mohabbat kaa udaayaa hai mazaaq!

Meri mehboob, kahin aur mila kar mujh se!

TAJ MAHAL

The Taj may be a symbol of love for you
And you may place faith in that verdant valley
But my love, please meet me elsewhere.

What is the meaning of the presence of the poor in
        these palaces?
On the paths, where the majesty of kings has been
        etched
Why should loving souls sojourn here?

My love, behind the curtain of exhibitionist romance
Do you not observe the marks of elitism?
You who are calmed in the mausoleums of dead kings
Could you not cast a look at your own dark house?

Countless people have fallen in love before
Who says their emotions were not authentic?
But this indelible memory is not for them
For they, like us, were poor.

This building, those tombs, these parapets, that fort
The signs of the grandeur of sovereign kings
Are like rose-hued writing on the face of this world
That has been coloured with the blood of your
     ancestors and mine.

My beloved, they too must have loved passionately
They—whose craft has given [the Taj] its beautiful
     visage
Their loved ones lie in unmarked graves
Where no one even lights a candle.

These gardens, these banks of the Jamuna, this palace
These intricately carved walls and doors and awnings
An emperor has used his immense wealth to mock the
     love of us poor.
My love, meet me anywhere but here.

2   QATAA

Vajh-e be rangi-e gulzaar kahoon to kya ho?
Kaun hai kitna gunahgaar, kahoon to kya ho?
Tum ne jo baat sar-e bazm na sun-na chaahi
Main wahi baat sar-e daar kahoon to kya ho?

QUATRAIN

What if I told you why the garden had no colour?
What if I outed those whose sins had caused this squalor?
Those words you do not wish whispered in civil soirées
What if those very words on the gallows I holler?

3   MAIN PAL DO PAL KA SHAYAR HOON

Main pal do pal ka shayar hoon
Pal do pal meri kahani hai
Pal do pal meri hasti hai
Pal do pal meri jawani hai

Mujh se pehle kitne shayar aaye aur aa kar chale gaye
Kuchh aahen bhar kar laut gaye kuchh naghme gaa
      kar chale gaye
Woh bhi ek pal ka qissa tha, main bhi ek pal ka qissa hoon
Kal tum se juda ho jaoonga, jo aaj tumhara hissa hoon

Har nasl ek fasl hai dharti ki, aaj uth-ti hai kal kat-ti hai
Jeevan vo mehngi midra hai, jo qatra qatra bat-ti hai
Pal do pal main ne sunaya hai, itni hi sa-aadat kaafi hai
Pal do pal tum ne mujh ko suna, itni hi inayat kaafi hai

Kal aur aayenge naghmon ki khilti kaliyan chunne wale
Mujh se behtar kahne wale tumse behtar sunne wale
Kal koi mujh ko yaad karey? Kyon koi mujh ko yaad
      karey?
Masroof zamaana mere liye kyon waqt apna barbaad
      karey?
Main pal do pal ka shayar hoon

I AM A POET OF A FEW MOMENTS

I am a poet of a few moments
And a few moments' worth is my story
A few moments' worth is my existence
And a few moments' worth is my youth.

Before me, so many poets came and went away
Some sighed in great anguish and left; others sang
    their songs and left too
They were the story of a few moments
I am a story of a few moments, too
Tomorrow, I'll be separated from you
Though I feel an integral part of you.

Every generation is a crop, grown today and
    harvested tomorrow
And life is that expensive liquor that is distributed by
    the drop
I have recited for a moment or two, this fortune is
    enough
You have listened for a moment or two, this favour
    too is enough.

Tomorrow, there will be others who will pluck the
    flowering buds of songs
Those who speak better than me, and those who
    listen better than you
Tomorrow, will someone remember me? Why at all
    should they remember me?
Why should this busy world waste its time for
    someone as inconsequential as me?
I am a poet of a few moments.

SULAIMAN KHATEEB

Main raste ki panti hoon, deepak hoon fan ka
Ye saara ujaala hai mere sukhan ka
Mujhe naich pehchaane logainch mere
Main anmol heera hoon Dakkan ki khan ka

I am the traveller of the path, I light the lamp of art
Through my dexterity this brightness do I impart
Alas, I remain unheeded! My people missed the signs
I am the invaluable gem of Deccan's diamond mines.

Sulaiman Khateeb (1922–78) was indeed a true gem from the mines of the Deccan, a Koh-i-noor. He was born in present-day Karnataka, and his family was steeped in devotion to Khwaja Banda Nawaaz, the patron saint of Gulbarga. Orphaned as a baby, he managed to channel his experiences of marginality into his poetry, and wrote evocatively about the poor and oppressed, including those trapped in moribund social institutions such as oppressed daughters-in-law, impoverished widows, financially strapped parents of girls facing dowry demands, and victims of sectarian riots. The most incredible part about Khateeb's work is that, despite its dark themes, it is witty—not smile-inwards witty, but roll-on-the-floor funny.[1] Despite his own precarious financial existence (he worked for the Karnataka State Water Works Department and yet won no patronage from the state),

Khateeb managed to hold his own as a poet of repute; despite his ability to write in traditional idioms (and his fluency in Persian), he treasured and nurtured the Dakkani style of speaking and writing in his work, legitimizing it in the eyes of a broader community of poets and listeners.

The poem I have translated is a small excerpt from a longer poem titled *Saas Bahu*, which is structured as a dialogue between a foul-mouthed, abusive and ignorant woman and her educated, urbane daughter-in-law who has no option but to listen to her mother-in-law's rants and reflect on her status. I wish I could have translated the whole poem with all its twists and turns; I hope this excerpt will provide a fleeting, partial sense of his turn of phrase and linguistic felicity.

SAAS BAHU

Saas:
Aanch ghar mein lagaa ko baithi hai
Ghar ka gampa gira ko baithi hai
Vo to potta sada ka deevana
Poora bandar banaa ko baithi hai . . .
Ujla dekha, uchhal gaya potta
Peela dekha, phisal gaya potta
Mere haatan se, kya karoon, amma
Saaf poora nikal gaya potta
Kaise jaale mein is ko pakdi hai
Admiyan khaane ki ek makdi hai

*Bahu (*Deevan-e Ghalib *ka ek safa ulat-te hue):*
Na suno gar bura kahe koi
Na kaho gar bura kahe koi
Rok lo gar ghalat chale koi

Bakhsh do gar khataa kare koi
Jab tavaqqo hi uth gaya Ghalib
Kyon kisi ka gila kare koi

Saas:
Kaun Ghalib, ye tera sagga hai?
Ki kaleje ko thham leti hai?
Itti deeda-dileri dekho ma!
Ghair mardon ka naam leti hai!

Bahu:
Baatein karti ho kis tarah ammi?
Baat heera hai baat moti hai
Baat lakhon ki laaj khoti hai
Baat har baat ko nahi kehte
Baat mushkil se baat hoti hai
Baat seene ka dagh hoti hai
Baat phoolon ka baagh hoti hai
Baat khair-o-sawaab hoti hai
Baat qahr-o-azaab hoti hai
Baat barg-e gulab hoti hai
Baat tegh-e itaab hoti hai
Baat kehte hain rabb-e arni ko
Baat ummul kitaab hoti hai
Baat bole kaleem ho jaye
Sun-ne wala nadeem hojaye
Baat khanjar ki kaat hoti hai!!

Saas:
Minje khanjar ki kaat boli na!
Minjhe kadhki so naat boli na!
Dikh ke murdon ki khaat boli na!
Ghud po pheke so taat boli na!
Minje chipkaa so chamboo boli na

Minje tadqaa so bamboo boli na!
Minje duniya ki kutni samjhee gey?
Laal mirchiyaan ki bukni samjhee gey?
Minje dammey ki dhuknee samjhee gey?
Minjhe phutti so phookni samjhee gey?
Marad aaney dey peet phodongee
Teri turbat banako ch'hodongi
Kitte jaatey hain tu bhi jaana gey
Aako khai-dast tujhe lejana gey
Ghis ke mirchiyan tujhe lagaana gey
Pooray peeraan ke haath jodonngee
Mitthe ghoday banaake ch'hodoongi
Ujlee shakkar ke chongay todoongi
Chaar nariyal mangaa ko phodoongi
Mere dil ko sukoon mil jayinga
Sukki daali pey phool khil jayinga

Bahu (aankhon mein aansoo laake):
Hum gharaane ki shaan rakhte hain
Band mutthi mein aan rakhte hain
Ghar ki izzat ka paas hai, varna
Hum bhi moonh mein zaban rakhte hain
Apni taleem rok leti hai
Baat badhte hi rok deti hai . . .

MOTHER-IN-LAW, DAUGHTER-IN-LAW

Mother-in-law:
She lit a fire in my house and relaxed
She broke our *gampa*[2] and relaxed
My son was always such an idiot
Now she has made him a monkey and she relaxed
He saw some white flesh and see how he slipped

He saw her ochre complexion and jumped
What can I say, friend, my own son
Is lost to me completely now
Look how she has ensnared him in her web
She is a man-eating spider, I tell you.

Daughter-in-law (turning the pages of the *Deevan-e
      Ghalib*):
Listen not if someone speaks ill
Speak not if someone speaks ill
Stop them if they go astray
Forgive those who bear ill-will
When expectation has been betrayed, Ghalib
How can one recriminate, still?

Mother-in-law:
Who, Ghalib? Is this a buddy of yours?
That you grab your heart with such feeling?
Look how forward is this wench, look
How she takes the name of unrelated men!

Daughter-in-law:
Why do you use such words, Ammi?
A word is a diamond, a word is a pearl
Not all words are worthy of being so termed
With difficulty, a word becomes a word
A word is a wound of the heart
A word is a garden of flowers
A word is a good deed, a blessing
A word is a curse, an epithet too
A word is the petal of a rose
And a sword of tyranny too
A word comes from God as well
A word is the mother of a book

The one who speaks can become a prophet
And a word can be a sword's cut too.

Mother-in-law:
Look, she called me a sword's cut
Look, she called me a cracked beam
Look, she called me a corpse's bier
Look, she called me a jute rug thrown on trash
Look, she called me a battered mug
Look, she called me a broken bamboo stick
Do you think I am a crushing tool, wench?
Do you think I am crushed chilli powder, wench?
Do you think I am an asthmatic's wheeze, wench?
Do you think I am a broken cylinder, wench?
Let my man come home, I will have your back broken
I will have your grave built today, just watch
So many die, why don't you die too, wench?
Contract diarrhoea, and shit and vomit to death, wench!
I should smear you with crushed chillies, wench
I will beg all the saints for your death
I will fry sweetmeats when you die
I will make desserts with confectioner's sugar
I will break four coconuts
I will be at peace at last
Like a dry branch that has suddenly flowered.

Daughter-in-law (tearing up):
I hold the dignity of the family dear
I hold our pride in my closed fist
The reputation of this house is our concern
Otherwise, I too harbour a tongue in my mouth
My education prevents me from replying
And stops me from escalating this conflict.

HABIB JALIB

Habib Jalib (1928–93), the Marxist-Leninist troubadour of Pakistan—a thorn in the flesh of every dictator, and a beacon of hope for the oppressed—was best known for his open mocking of Zia-ul Haq (playing with his name 'Zia', which means light, and contrasting it with the word *zulmat*, meaning darkness):

> *Zulmat ko 'Zia', sarsar ko saba, bande ko khuda kya*
> *   likhna? Kya likhna?*
> *Patthar ko gohar, deewaar ko dar, jugnu ko diyaa kya*
> *   likhna? Kya likhna?*

> Why write that darkness is light, that a rustle is the
>   breeze,
> That a human is God? Why?
> Why call a stone a jewel, a wall a door, or call a firefly a
>   lamp? Why?

His reward for such verses was long spells in jail under every possible dictator imaginable. His defiant verse must be read by imagining its context—that of a poet who was fully aware of the consequences of each public performance; and that of a person who had been incarcerated in brutal conditions, and would, after being released, immediately call attention to the oppressiveness of his interlocutors, and ready himself for another period in prison.

A longish documentary containing Jalib's interviews and a few performances are available in the public domain on YouTube. The documentary showcases his personal bravery, and contains the poems I have translated below. Also, a very competent translation of ten of Jalib's poems—of which I would highly recommend '*Maulaana*'—can also be found online.[1] The second poem I have included here contains Jalib's avowal that his repudiation of traditional romantic themes is a personal choice: note the penultimate sher where he privileges the '*dahr ke gham*' (the pain of the world) over '*sarv qaamat ki javaani*' (the beauty of youth).

1   **DASTOOR**

Deep jis ka mahallat hi mein jale
Chand logon ki khushiyon ko le kar chale
Vo jo saaye mein har maslehat ke pale
Aise dastoor ko, subh-e benoor ko
Main nahin maanta! Main nahin jaanta.

Main bhi kharij nahin takhta-e daar se
Main bhi Mansoor hoon, keh do aghyaar se
Kyon daraate ho zindaan ki deewaar se
Zulm ki baat ko, jahl ki raat ho
Main nahin maanta! Main nahin jaanta.

Tum kaho phool shaaqon pe khilne lage
Tum kaho jaam rindon ko milne lage
Tum kaho chaak seenon ke silne lage
Is khule jhoot ko zehn ki loot ko
Main nahin maanta! Main nahin jaanta.

Tum ne loota hai sadiyon hamaara sukoon
Ab na hum par chalega tumhara fusoon
Charagar dardmandon ke bante ho kyon
Tum nahin chaaragar, log mane magar
Main nahin maanta! Main nahin jaanta.

I DO NOT ABIDE!

That which lights lamps only in palaces
That which caters to the whims of elite classes
That flourishes in the shadow of all compromises
Such a system, such a light-starved dawn
I do not agree with! I do not abide!

I am not to be excluded from the scaffold
I am Mansoor[2] too, let the outsiders know
And how dare you scare me with talk of dungeons
This talk of tyranny, this ignorance dark as night
I do not agree with! I do not abide!

You tell me that flowers are blooming on trees
You tell me that the thirsty have found wine at
                taverns
You tell me that the tattered robes are now stitched
This open lie, this robbery of the senses
I do not agree with! I do not abide!

You have robbed us of our peace for centuries
But your spell has now been broken finally
Do not pretend to be the healer of wounds
You are no physician, others may believe you so, but
I do not agree! I do not abide!

2   AUR SAB BHOOL GAYE

Aur sab bhool gaye, harf-e sadaaqat likhna
Reh gaya kaam hamaara hi baghaavat likhna

Laakh kahte rahen zulmat ko na zulmat likhna
Hum ne seekha hi nahin pyaare ba-ijaazat likhna

Na sile ki na sitaish ki tamanna hum ko[3]
Haq mein logon ke hamaari to hai aadat likhna

Hum ne jo bhool ke bhi shah ka qaseeda na likha
Shaayad aayaa isi khoobi ki badaulat likhna

Us se badh kar meri tehseen bhalaa kya hogi
Padh ke naakhush hain mera saaheb-e sarvat likhna

Dahr ke gham se hua rabt to hum bhool gaye
Sarv qaamat ki javaani ko qayaamat likhna

Kuchh bhi kahte hain kahein shah ke masaahib, Jalib
Rang rakhna yahi apna isi soorat likhna

OTHERS FORGOT

All others forgot to defend the word of truth, alas
To write of revolution, I was left alone at last

'Do not write that nights are dark,' they warned me in
        their fear
But I never sought to write with permission, my dear

[Like Ghalib] I crave no reward nor desire praise
But in support of the downtrodden, my voice I raise

Not even by oversight sang I an ode to the king
Perhaps this adds rhythm to my poems when I sing

What greater acclamation could this poet hope for?
Than that my writings annoyed those that were in
      power

I admit that I forgot amid this stark oppression
To write of youthful beauty, and call it devastation

Jalib, the king's courtiers are free to say what they feel
None can hide the crimson colour my poems reveal.[4]

MUSTAFA ZAIDI

Inhi pathharon pe chal kar agar aa sako to aao
Mere ghar ke raaste mein koi kahkashaan nahi hai

If you wish to come, you must take the stony road
The stars do not light up the way to my abode.

Mustafa Zaidi (1930–70) died young, and the circumstances of his death were lurid, involving extramarital liaisons, a suicide pact with a lover who survived, and dark accusations of murder. Rather unfortunately, these issues have tended to overshadow discussions about his considerable talent. Zaidi should have been seen as one of the stalwarts of the progressive movement in Pakistan in the 1960s, but his due has mostly eluded him, partly because of the rather colourful posthumous publicity that enveloped him.

Zaidi's first book, *Raushni*, was published when he was merely nineteen years old, and still in India. He moved to Pakistan in the early 1950s, and after a brief stint in academia, went on to become a senior civil servant. His career ended badly when he was dismissed during Yahya Khan's purge of 303 bureaucrats in 1970. His death shortly after led to the murder trial of his paramour, which assumed the status of a media circus. During that time, several literary journals brought out special issues on his work. Eventually, his *Kulliyaat* (complete works) was published in the

211

mid 1970s, which also included some of the most superlative praise of his work by Faiz, Firaaq and Josh.[1]

I have chosen to translate two brief works. The first is a ghazal that has been sung by Abida Parveen, among others, while the second is an excerpt from his luminous poem '*Koh-e Nida*' (hat tip to my friend Jaffar Naqvi for introducing me to this poem, and to Zaidi). The imagery of the Koh-e Nida is from the Arabian folk tale of Hatim Tai in which a mountain called out to people, who upon entering it were consumed by it. Written at the tail end of Zaidi's life, this poem has been interpreted by many as a poetic suicide note, where Zaidi sees the world as a beckoning killer mountain.

1   AANDHI CHALI

> Aandhi chali to naqsh-e kaf-e paa nahin mila
> Dil jis se mil gaya vo dobaraa nahin mila

> Aavaaz ko to kaun samajhta ke door door
> Khaamoshiyon ka dard-shanasaa nahin mila

> Hum anjuman mein sab ki taraf dekhte rahe
> Apni tarah se koi akela nahin mila

> Kachche ghade ne jeet li naddi chadhi hui
> Mazboot kashtiyon ko kinara nahin mila

THE STORM

So intense was the storm, even footprints were wiped
out

To lose those I desired—that's been my fate
    throughout

Who could have recognized that voice, no one had the
    gift
That could feel the painful cadence of a silent shout

I locked eyes with everyone in that public soirée
Alas I found none as lonely as me, without a doubt

The clay pitcher survived the swells of flooded rivers
It reached the shore, while the storm shattered ships
    strong and stout.

2   **KOH-E NIDA**

Ayyohan-naas chalo koh-e nida ki jaanib

Kab tak aashufta-sari hogi naye naamon se
Thhak chuke honge kharabaat ke hangaamon se
Har taraf ek hi andaz mein din dhalte hain
Log har shehr mein saaye ki tarah chalte hain
Ajnabi khauf ko seenon mein chhupaae hue log
Apne aaseb ke taaboot uthaaye hue log
Zaat ke karb mein bazaar ki rusvaai mein
Tum bhi shamil ho is anboh ki tanhaai mein

Tum bhi ek baadiya paimaa ho khala ki jaanib
Ayyohan-naas chalo koh-e nida ki jaanib

Raat bhar jaagte rehte hain dukaanon ke charaagh
Dil vo sunsaan jazeera, ke bujha rehta hai

Lekin is band jazeere hi ke ek goshe mein
Zaat ka baab-e tilismaat khula rehta hai
Apni hi zaat mein pasti ke khandar milte hain
Apni hi zaat mein ek koh-e nida rehta hai
Sirf us koh ke daaman mein mayassar hai najaat
Aadmi varna anaasir mein ghira rehta hai
Aur phir in se bhi ghabra ke uthaata hai nazar

Apne mazhab ki taraf, apne khuda ki jaanib
Ayyohan-naas chalo koh-e nida ki jaanib

THE CALLING MOUNTAIN

My fellow humans, let's go answer the mountain's call.

How long will we use new names to conceal our distress?
You too must be tired of this misfortune and stress
Everywhere the new day brings similar tired woes
In each city folk move strangely like zombie shadows
In their hearts they conceal strange fears camouflaged
            as cares
Demons disguised as idols, this strange multitude bears
Private pains of existence, the market's public shame
Don't you judge this crowd, you too have played this
            lonely game

Like barren promises, into this void let us fall
My fellow humans, let's go answer the mountain's call.

The bright lamps of shops stay lit all night, garish and
            stark
The heart, though, is that silent island that remains dark

But in every corner of this island, near and far
The magic door of selfhood remains open, ajar
In our self, we see lowly ruins of hurt and pain
In our own self we see the cursed beckoning mountain
In that mountain's caves—that is where our salvation
    lies
Else humans stay trapped in webs of relations and ties
And fearful of those too, they slowly raise up their eyes

They summon their God, enveloped in religious thrall
My fellow humans let's go answer the mountain's call.

AHMED FARAZ

Ahmed Faraz (1931–2008) wrote such exquisite Urdu ghazals that it is almost impossible to believe that he was not a native speaker but rather a Pashtoon who grew up speaking Hindko. Like Jalib, he too suffered incarceration and exile under the Zia-ul Haq regime, but continued to write critically about the regime. Unlike Jalib's plebeian verses though, Faraz favoured highly stylized language in his compositions.

In a rehabilitation of sorts, Faraz was feted in his later years, and even awarded the prestigious *Hilal-e Imtiaz* by the government in 2004. However, in 2006, in protest against Pervez Musharraf's anti-democratic policies, Faraz returned the award, and died in 2008, unheralded by institutional awards but with a unique place in the hearts of Pakistanis, Urdu-lovers and lovers of freedom of expression everywhere. The public domain contains many of his performances, including the famous '*Mohaasara*' ('Siege'), written in direct defiance of Zia-ul Haq.[1] The poem describes a besieged individual under attack from a powerful army, which sends him an invitation to surrender, to which he predictably responds defiantly.

The first ghazal[2] I have translated here (a traditional poem, but one for which he got some flak from conservatives for a direct reference to nudity) stands in stark contrast to the heartbreaking lyricism of Faraz's best-known ghazal, '*Ranjish hi sahi*'[3]. I include that ghazal along with two more snippets from Faraz's poetry.

1   **SUNAA HAI**

> *Sunaa hai log use aankh bhar ke dekhte hain*
> *So uske shahr mein kuchh din thahar ke dekhte hain*

> *Sunaa hai rabt hai us ko kharaab haalon se*
> *So apne aap ko barbaad kar ke dekhte hain*

> *Sunaa hai us ko bhi hai sher-o-shaayiri se sharaf*
> *So hum bhi mojize apne hunar ke dekhte hain*

> *Sunaa hai bole so baton se phool jhadte hain*
> *Ye baat hai to chalo, baat kar ke dekhte hain*

> *Sunaa hai us ke shabistaan se muttasil hai bahisht*
> *Makeen udhar ke bhi jalve idhar ke dekhte hain*

> *Kise naseeb ke be-pairahan use dekhen*
> *Kabhi kabhi dar-o-deevar ghar ke dekhte hain*

> *Ab us ke shahr mein thehren, ke kooch kar jaayen*
> *Faraz aao, sitaare safar ke dekhte hain*

IT HAS BEEN SAID

> My love is the cynosure of eyes, everyone says
> Why not stay in this city for just a few more days?

> They say that the bereft receive his consideration
> Let us destroy ourselves in this anticipation

It has been said that good poetry is close to his heart
So let us try to showcase miracles of our art

They say when my lover speaks, flowers fall from
their stalks
Let us speak then, and see what transpires in our talks

Across from my lover's bedroom, they say heaven lies
Dwellers of the other side this way have cast their eyes

Who is fortunate enough to see my lover nude?
Only his walls and roof, that too rarely, we conclude

Should we stay in my lover's city, or should we pass?
Let us leave that decision to the stars, dear Faraz.

2   CHAND NAADAAN, CHAND DEEVANE

Raat ke jaan-gudaaz zulmat mein
Azm ki mashaalen jalaaye hue
Dil mein le kar baghaawaton ke sharaar
Vahshaton ke muheeb saaye mein
Sar-bakaf, jaan-ba lab, nigaah-ba qasr
Surkh-o-khooni alam uthhaaye hue
Badh rahe hain junoon ke aalam mein
Chand naadaan, chand deevane

A FEW PASSIONATE NOVICES

In the murderous darkness
Having lit the torches of their determination

Carrying sparks of rebellion in their hearts
In the intimidating shadows of danger
Heads high, lives in the balance, and eyes on the palace
Carrying red, bloodstained banners
They march with frenzy
A few passionate novices.

3 RANJISH HI SAHI

Ranjish hi sahi, dil hi dukhaane ke liye aa
Aa phir se mujhe chhod ke jaane ke liye aa

Pehle se maraasim na sahi phir bhi kabhi to
Rasm-o-rah-e duniya hi nibhaane ke liye aa

Kis kis ko bataayenge judaai ka sabab hum
Tu mujh se khafaa hai to zamaane ke liye aa

Kuchh to mere pindaar-e muhabbat ka bharam rakh
Tu bhi to kabhi mujh ko manaane ke liye aa

Ek umr se hoon lazzat-e giriyaa se bhi mehroom
Ai raahat-e jaan, mujh ko rulaane ke liye aa

Ab tak dil-e khush-fahm ko tujh se hain ummeeden
Ye aakhri sham-en bhi bujhaane ke liye aa

BE IT UNPLEASANTNESS ALONE

Be it unpleasantness alone, just to hurt my heart, come
Come if only to reprise your spurning and leave, come

I know our relations are no longer what they were
But to fulfil empty social obligations, won't you come?

How many times should I explain why we chose to part?
Be angry with me, but for appearances' sake, do come

For once at least allow your lover one moment of pride
For once let me be angry, and to placate me, come

For an age, I have been deprived of the sweetness of grief
O solace of my life! Even to make me weep, do come

My foolish optimistic heart still harbours hopes of you
This last lamp remains lit, to extinguish it, please do come.

GULZAR

Gulzar (b. 1934) has served Urdu in multiple ways. His film songs have always been infused with the most elaborate of Persianized rhythms that jostle with more Sanskritic patterns to produce the true Ganga–Jamuna effect of Urdu. His metaphors are unique—my favourite is '*ek baar waqt se, lamha gira kahin*' ('once a moment fell from time'), invoking a leaf falling from a tree.[1] He has also written several non-film poems and short stories in Urdu; his anthology *Raavi Paar* (Across the Raavi River) is especially notable, as is his recent collection titled *Neglected Poems*, which elevates the quotidian to poetic heights. In addition, he has served the cause of Urdu poetry through his magnificent 1988 TV serial *Mirza Ghalib*, which was the entry point to the work of Ghalib for a new generation.

Gulzar has won seven National Awards, twenty Filmfare trophies, the Sahitya Akademi Award and the Padma Bhushan. His song '*Jai Ho*' won the Oscar for best lyrics in 2009. He currently serves as the chancellor of Assam University, and was awarded the Indira Gandhi Award for National Integration in 2012.

I have included three non-film poems here, and one film-based composition, which in my opinion exemplifies the innovative language he deploys in his verse.[2]

1   **TANHAA**

> *Zindagi yoon hui basar tanhaa*
> *Qaafila saath, aur safar tanhaa*
>
> *Apne saaye se chaunk jaate hain*
> *Umr guzri hai is qadar tanhaa*
>
> *Raat bhar bolte hain sannaate*
> *Raat kaate koi kidhar tanhaa*
>
> *Din guzartaa nahin hai logon mein*
> *Raat hoti nahin basar tanhaa*
>
> *Hum ne darvaze tak to dekhaa tha*
> *Phir na jaane gaye kidhar tanhaa*

ALONE

> Thus I led my life solitary, alone
> The caravan alongside, the journey alone
>
> Startled am I by my own shadow
> I have spent my days to this degree alone
>
> All night long, they speak to me
> The silences, they never leave me alone
>
> Though I cannot abide people by day
> I'm loath to spend nights sans company, alone
>
> I saw them off at my doorway and then
> They left, and went on their odyssey alone.

2 AADATAN

Aadatan tum ne kar diye vaade
Aadatan hum ne aitbaar kiya

Teri raahon mein baar-haa ruk kar
Hum ne apnaa hi intezaar kiya

Ab na maangenge zindagi yaarab
Ye gunaah hum ne ek baar kiya

SHEER HABIT

Out of sheer habit, you made a promise
And similarly, habitually, I trusted you

Tarrying continually by your paths
I kept on awaiting myself, I guess

Never again will I seek life, O Lord
I have made this mistake once; that is enough.

3 IS MOD SE JAATE HAIN

Is mod se jaate hain
Kuchh sust-qadam raste, kuchh tez-qadam raahen
Patthar ki haveli ko, sheeshe ke gharaundon mein
Tinkon ke nasheman tak, is mod se jaate hain

Aandhi ki tarah ud kar, ek raah guzarti hai
Sharmaati hui koyi qadmon se utarti hai

In reshmi raahon mein, ek raah to woh hogi
Tum tak jo pahunchti hai
Is mod se jaati hai

Ek door se aati hai, paas aake palat-ti hai
Ek raah akeli si, rukti hai na chalti hai
Ye soch ke baithhi hoon, ek raah to woh hogi
Tum tak jo pahunchti hai
Is mod se jaati hai

FROM THIS BEND IN THE ROAD

From this bend in the road
Go some slow-paced paths
And some fast highways
To the stone palace, the glasshouse and the nest of
        little debris
All paths go from this bend.

One path flies along like a hurricane
Another moves with shy footsteps
On these velvet roads, there must be at least one path
That reaches you; that too starts from this bend.

One path comes from really far away, and turns just
        as it reaches here
And one path, alone, neither stops nor moves
And I sit here, thinking, there must be at least one
        path
That reaches you
That too starts from this bend in the road.

4   MAKAAN KI OOPRI MANZIL PE AB KOI NAHIN REHTA

Makaan ki oopri manzil pe ab koi nahin rehta
Vo kamre band hain kab se
Vo chaubi seedhiyaan un tak pahunchti thhin
Vo ab oopar nahin jaatin

Makaan ki oopri manzil pe ab koi nahin rehta
Vahaan kamron mein itna yaad hai mujh ko
Khilone ek purani tokri mein bhar ke rakhe the
Bahut se to uthhane phenkne rakhne mein choor ho
    gaye

Vahaan ek balcony bhi thhi
Jahaan ek beth ka jhoola latakta thha
Mera ek dost thha tota
Vo roz aata thha, us ko hari mirchi khilaata thha
Usi ke saamne chhat thhi
Jahaan ek mor baitha aasmaan pe raat bhar
Meethe sitaare chugta rehta thha

Mere bachhon ne vo dekha nahi
Vo neeche ki manzil pe rehte hain
Jahaan par piano rakha hai
Purane Parsi style ka
(Fraser se khareeda thha)
Magar kuchh besuri aavaazen karta hai
Ke us ki reeds saari hil gayi hain
Suron par doosre sur chhad gaye hain

Usi manzil pe ek pushtaini baithak thhi
Jahaan purkhon ki tasveeren latakti rehti theen
Main seedha karta thha, havaa phir tedha kar jaati

Bahu ko moochhon vale saare purkhe cliché lagte the
Mere bachhon ne aakhir un ko keelon se utaara
Purane newspaper mein unhe mehfooz kar ke rakh
    diya thha
Mera ek bhaanja le jaata hai filmon mein kabhi
Set par lagaata hai
Kiraya milta hai un se

Meri manzil pe mere saamne mehmaan-khaana hai
Mere potay kabhi Amreeka se aayen to rukte hain
Alag size mein aate hain vo jitni baar aate hain
Khuda jaane vohi aate hain ya har baar koi doosra
    aata hai

Vo ek kamra jo peeche ki taraf band hai
Jahaan batti nahin jalti
Vahaan ek rosary rakhi hai, vo us se mehakta hai
Vahaan vo dayi rehti thhi
Jis ne teen bachhon ko bada karne mein
Apni umr de di thhi
Mari to main ne dafnaaya nahin
Mehfooz kar ke rakh diya us ko

Aur us ke baad, ek do seedhiyan hain
Neeche tehkhaane mein jaati hai
Jahaan khamoshi raushan hai
Sukoon soya hua hai

Bas itni si pehloo mein jagah rakh kar
Ke jab main seedhiyon se neechen aaoon
To usi ke pehloon mein baazoo pe sar rakh kar
Gale lag jaaoon
So jaaoon

Makaan ki oopri manzil pe ab koi nahin rehta

NO ONE LIVES ON THE TOP FLOOR OF THE HOUSE ANY MORE

No one lives on the top floor of the house any more
Those rooms have long been shut
The wooden staircase that reached them
Has decayed.

No one lives on the top floor of the house any more
In those rooms, I do remember,
Was an old basket full of toys
Many must be crushed by now in the constant
    moving and shifting.

There was a balcony there
Where a wicker-swing swung,
A parrot friend of mine
Used to swoop down and I would feed it a green chilli
And there was the rooftop, right there
Where a peacock used to sit
And eat sweet stars from the sky all night long.

My children never saw all that
They used to live on the lower level
Where there used to be a piano
Old Parsi style
(We had bought it from Fraser's)
But now it makes strange sounds
For all its reeds are now shaken up
And on old tunes, some new tunes have mounted.

On that level, there was an old ceremonial drawing
    room

Where the photos of the ancestors used to hang
I used to straighten them out, only for the wind to
    make them crooked again
My daughter-in-law always found the mustachioed
    ancestors to be clichés
My children finally took those pictures down from
    those nails
And wrapped them in old newspapers
My nephew sometimes takes them to movie sets
Rents them out for money.

On my floor, there is a guest-room in front of mine
When my grandchildren visit from America, they stay
    there
Every time they come, they are a different size
God knows if the same children come, or if there are
    different ones every time!

There is a room at the back, closed
No light shines there
It has a rosary, which exudes fragrance
A nanny used to live there
Who, while raising my three children,
Gave away her whole life
When she died, I did not bury her
But kept her safe there.

And then, there are a few stairs
That descend into a basement
Silence shines there
And peace is asleep.

With just enough room
That when I descend those stairs
I should find room to nestle into it
Embrace it
And fall asleep.

No one lives on the top floor of the house any more.

SHAHRYAR

Akhlaq Muhammad Khan Shahryar (1936–2012) is best known in the popular realm for his film songs in the 1981 movie *Umrao Jaan*, which in my opinion is a matter of repute, given their poetic quality. However, he must also be celebrated as an academic and a philosopher, who headed the Urdu Department at the Aligarh Muslim University and edited *Sher-o-Hikmat* (Poetry and Philosophy), a prestigious Urdu journal. He published several books of poetry, and is the only Urdu poet to have won both the Sahitya Akademi Award (1987) and the Jnanpith Award (2008). His death in February 2012 robbed Urdu literature of a classical talent, one whose deep philosophical insights never compromised the poetic quality of his nazms.[1]

I have translated two of his poems here, both of which made their way into the film world. The first, '*Seene mein jalan*', is a marvellous poetic rendition of urban anomie, and is featured in the 1978 movie *Gaman*. It was set to music beautifully by Jaidev and sung by Suresh Wadkar. The second ghazal was immortalized in *Umrao Jaan*, wonderfully rendered by Asha Bhonsle and aided by Khayyam's music.

1   SEENE MEIN JALAN

> *Seene mein jalan, aankhon mein toofan sa kyon hai*
> *Is shahr mein har shakhs pareshaan sa kyon hai*

Dil hai to dhadakne ka bahaana koi dhoonde
Patthar ki tarah behis-o-bejaan sa kyon hai

Tanhaai ki ye kaun si manzil hai rafeeqo
Taa hadd-e nazar ek bayaaban sa kyon hai

Hum ne to koi baat nikaali nahin gham ki
Vo zood pashemaan pashemaan sa kyon hai

Kya koi nayi baat nazar aati hai hum mein
Aaina hamen dekh ke hairaan sa kyon hai

HEART AFIRE

Why is the heart aflame, why do eyes harbour a
    storm?
Why does everyone in this city appear forlorn?

If there be a heart, it should seek reasons to beat on
Why is it so lifeless and unfeeling like a stone?

What is this stage of empty solitude, my dear friend?
Why do my eyes see naught but a desert end to end?

I hadn't brought up an issue melancholy or sad
Why does that quick repenter appear to feel bad?

My face reflects something strange, perhaps a hurt
    that's new?
For the mirror appears surprised at my visage too.

2   IN AANKHON KI MASTI

In aankhon ki masti ke mastaane hazaaron hain
In aankhon se vaabastaa afasaane hazaaron hain

Ek tum hi nahin tanhaa ulfat mein meri rusvaa
Is shahr mein tum jaise deevane hazaaron hain

Ek sirf hami mai ko aankhon se pilaate hain
Kehne ko to duniyaa mein maikhaane hazaaron hain

Is sham-e farozan ko aandhi se daraate ho
Is sham-e farozan ke parvaane hazaaron hain

THESE FANCIFUL EYES

These eyes have caught the fancy of dreamers' dreams
   a thousand times
Yes, these eyes have been linked with stories and
   themes a thousand times

It is not you alone who has been destroyed by this lost
   love
My beauty has foiled many a lover's schemes a
   thousand times

I am that unique cupbearer who serves wine by the eyeful
This unique tavern drives drinkers to extremes a
   thousand times

How dare you try and scare this flame with your talk
   of the tempest
This flame has won suicidal moths' last esteems a
   thousand times.

ASIF RAZA

Chand pe jaa kar raushan raushan patthar lane waale log
Kitne thande thande hain ye aag churaane wale log

They who go to the moon, and bring back bright, shiny stones
How cold indeed are these people of the fire-stealer clan![1]

Asif Raza (b. 1942) comes from a family of poets. His father, Manzoor Hussain Shore, was a part of Aligarh's golden generation, and a respected poet of the progressive tradition. Raza, however, inhabits a different aesthetic, more akin to French symbolists like Baudelaire and the surrealists, and exhibits hints of German existentialist influences, particularly from Friedrich Nietzsche and Karl Jaspers. He taught sociology in the United States; but after the runaway success of his 2008 collection of poems *Bujhe Rangon ki Raunaq* (The Splendour of Faded Colours) and his recent retirement, his poetry has enjoyed a renaissance of sorts and he is at work on a new collection.

The poem I have translated here reflects the strong European and surrealist influence in Raza's poetry, where on a coral island (a symbol of transcendental beauty rather than a quotidian existence), seven beautiful women live trapped, watching the crashing waves mock their confinement, as they try to lure sailors to the island. But the mystery of the island and the impossible beauty of the seven sisters paradoxically strike terror in the heart

233

of the pusillanimous sailors who hear them, rather than evoking desire, thus accentuating the disjuncture between the two worlds. The non-linear construction of the poem lends itself to multiple interpretations, each one as disquieting as the previous.

SAAT BEHNEN

Ek marjaani jazeere par, areez
Saat behnen, shabkharaami ki mareez
Subah-dam, khwaab-e shabaana ke ta-aaqub mein
     davaan
Ek sang-e surkh ko apna banaa kar deedban
Jaaiza pur-shauq leti hain khalaa-e bahr ka
Phailta hai jhaag sahil par palat-ti lehr ka

Qad kasheeda saat behnon ke sunehre baal hain
Kapkapaate baakira lab laal hain
Tegh jaisa abruon ka un ke mehraabi hai kham
Mauj-zan seenon mein ek toofan hai na-mukhtatum
Hadd-e faasil khenchti dehleez-e aab
Eestaada dekhti rehti hain khwaab

Kaundti hain in ki aankhon mein jawaahar ki chamak
Shaahraah-e aab lekin be-lachak
Dekhti hain vo ke na aabaad hai, tasveer-e yaas
Door uftaada ufaq par baadbaan ka iltebaas!
Muthiyon se un ke girte hain samandar ke aqeeq
Qa'ar leta hai jinhe vaapas, ameeq

Barbat-e zarreen utha kar haft taar
Chhedti hain vo tilaai shaahkar

Goonjti un ki sawaahil par sada sat-sargami
Neelgoon choti pe apni baad-e khezan hai thami
Sun ke un ka geet istemraar mein
Be-sada aabi jaras hai, ghaar mein

Baaz-gashtaana hai un ke purghina paighaam mein
Aab-e nuqradar ka vaada tilaai jaam mein
Lamha-e Iqbal ka muzhda (bataur-e armaghan
Pesh karta hai sadaf moonh dhaanp kar la'al-e giraan)
Ediyan un ki gulaabi choom kar jal ki tahen
Barhami khote hue apni thamein

Ek zarreen rau ke istefsaar par
Sar-nigoon ho kar chatakti hai chataanon ki kagar
Varta-e majhool ki na-vaqifi
Pech aabi khol ke karta hua apni nafi
Munhamik bizzaat ek itlaaf mein hai mubtela
Subha sath-e aab ko deti hui rang-e tila
Neelgoon gehraaiyon hain un ki aankhon ki attah
Taif ghaltaan jin mein lete hain panaah
Nuqrai shaakhon se zarreen seb seenon par dhare
Dekhti rehti hain kohre ke pare
Sahil-e dahshat se lekin ehteraaz
Aabna-e bahr mein daakhil nahin koi jahaaz

Simt-e manzil hai khamoshi se ravaan
Taajiron ka kaarbardaari se bojhal kaarvaan
Haath mathon par tikaye, raah kosh
Kaalbud mastool par hain, tez chashm-o-tez gosh
Zer-e lab sargoshiyon mein zikr-e bandargaah hai
Pesh been rooh-e amal hai, isteraahat khwah hai

SEVEN SISTERS

On a vast coral island
Seven sisters, somnambulist,
As the day dawns, pursue their nightly dreams
A red rock becomes their lookout
As they gaze at the wide expanse of the ocean
And espy no more than the foam of returning waves.

Tall of stature, and blond, all seven
Their virgin red lips aquiver
Their eyebrows arched like scimitars
An unending storm rages in their breasts
The threshold of the waterfront marks their limit
All that breaches it is their dream.

Their eyes suddenly sparkle like diamonds
But alas, the highway of water is desolate
Their eyes resume their bleak expression
As the hint of a sail recedes from their view
The rubies they hold fall from their hands
Which return into unquestioning depths.

They pick up their golden lyres, with the seven strings
And sing their golden masterpiece
Their seven-octaved voices reach the shores
On the blue-tipped mountaintops, the wind stops
The watery bell stops ringing in its cave.

Their returning song carries promises of untold riches
Of golden chalices bearing silvery draughts
And intimations of eternal moments
(A seashell shyly promises a priceless pearl)

The waves touch their pink heels
And are rendered silent.

As if responding to a question from an undertow
The craggy cliff bows its head and shatters
A maelstrom announces its ignorance
By unspooling its watery negations;
As if engaged in a ritual of self-ruination
The morning scatters its gold on the surface of the sea.

In the blue depths of their eyes
Only ghosts seek sanctuary
Silver apples pressed to their bosoms
They peer toward the foggy horizon in expectation
But terror-struck sailors
Enter not the bay.

Toward its destination, bears on silently,
A caravan of trading ships, laden with commodities
Hands on foreheads, tracing a straight course
The dark silhouettes sharp of eyes and ears
In whispers speak of a known harbour
And the promise of rest
Before their journey to another harbourage.

IFTIKHAR ARIF

Iftikhar Arif (b. 1943) was born in India, and moved to Pakistan in 1965. His first book, *Mehr-e Doneem* (Sliced Moon), was published in 1983, and his most recent book, *Kitab-e Dil-o-Duniya* (The Book of the Heart and the World), in 2009. He has won a variety of literary awards, including the prestigious *Hilal-e Imtiaz* in 2005. He is also a well-known literary critic, whose work on Faiz has garnered praise.

Arif's work cuts across genres, as my two selections here show.[1] In the first, Arif produces a qaseeda in praise of Imam Husain (the figure of the Battle of Karbala), who is very popular among Shias, and among Urdu-lovers. The last sher here is significant, because it conjures up a sense of Husain's power as one who can intercede on behalf of sinners. In two lines, the poet is able to sketch a complex scenario. We are introduced to a moment during the Day of Judgement, where Ali intercedes on the poet's behalf to Prophet Mohammed, also known as the *shafa-e mehshar* (one who will heal on Judgement Day), imploring the Prophet to let Arif into heaven, because, despite being a sinner, he belongs to Husain.

In stark contrast, the second selection is a straight-up poem constituting a lover's wish-list. In it, Arif deftly juxtaposes irony with desire to produce a confessional effect.

1   SHARAF KE SHAHR MEIN

Sharaf ke shahr mein har baam-o-dar Husain ka hai
Zamaane bhar ke gharaanon mein ghar Husain ka hai

Kahaan ki jang, kahaan jaa ke sar hui hai ke ab
Tamaam aalam-e khair-o-khabar Husain ka hai

Zameen kha gayi kya kya buland baala darakht
Hara bhara hai jo ab bhi, shajar Husain ka hai

Savaal bayat-e shamsheer par javaaz bahut
Magar jawaab wahi mo'tabar Husain ka hai

Muhabbaton ke havaalon mein zikr aane lagaa
Ye fazl bhi to mere haal par Husain ka hai

'Huzoor Shaafa-e mehshar,' Ali kahen ke ye shakhs
'Gunaahgaar bahut hai magar Husain ka hai'

IN THE CITY OF PRIVILEGE

In the city of privilege, every roof and wall belongs to
    Husain
Of all clans, there is none like the house that belongs
    to Husain

When was this war fought, when was it won?
    Someone say!

For it appears that all this world of good belongs to
Husain

The earth has long since swallowed such big forests
but still
The lush and verdant tree is the one that belongs to
Husain

The question of obeisance was made legitimate by the
sword
But the reply, confident and courageous, belongs to
Husain

That my name began to crop up in legends of love
This bestowal on my being also belongs to Husain

On Judgement Day, Ali will speak to Mohammed and say
'Pardon him; though a great sinner, this one belongs
to Husain.'

2 **DAYAAR-E NOOR MEIN**

Dayaar-e noor mein teera-shabon ka saathi ho
Koi to ho jo meri vahshaton ka saathi ho

Main us se jhooth bhi boloon to mujh se sach bole
Mere mizaaj ke sab mausamon ka saathi ho

Vo mere naam ki nisbat se mo'tabar thehre
Gali gali meri rusvaaiyon ka saathi ho

Main us ke haath na aaoon vo mera hoke rahe
Main gir padoon to meri pastiyon ka saathi ho

Vo khvaab dekhe to dekhe mere havaale se
Mere khayaalon ke sab manzaron ka saathi ho

IN THESE MOMENTS OF LIGHT

> In these moments of light, a friend for darker days I
> seek
> Someone to comfort me during my panicked phase I
> seek
>
> Even if I lie constantly, he should speak naught but
> truth
> A mate for all my capricious moods and ways, I seek
>
> His fortitude should outlast my golden 'glory days'
> His support, when I lie forlorn in a shamed haze, I
> seek
>
> I may become elusive but he should remain mine
> If I fall to abjection, his arms to raise me, I seek
>
> If he must dream, all his fancies should have me as
> referent
> That my wonder and delight should leave him
> amazed, I seek.

S.M. SHAHED

Syed Mohammed Shahed (b. 1944) exemplifies the neorealist tradition of progressive Urdu poetry in its most raw form, with sweeping broadsides against organized religion, class prejudice and unreason. He sacrifices the rigour of rhyme and metre for a naked directness that brings to mind the works of Soviet modernists like Mayakovsky, and the early Pablo Neruda.

Trained as a mechanical engineer, Shahed kept his craft on hold during his career, but his art has seen a blossoming since his retirement. His work is archived online at the website UrduShahkar[1], where he has included several translations of progressive poets along with his own work. My favourite is the set of painstaking translations of the marsiyas of Josh Malihabadi, who had used the stories of Imam Husain as metaphors for contemporary social issues. Shahed's translations are works of painstaking annotation, reminding one of Martin Gardner's translations of the works of Lewis Carroll.

Here, I have translated one of Shahed's recent poems *'Fikr'* ('Thought'). In this poem, he links the Abrahamic sacrifice of his son, a cornerstone of Islamic and Judeo-Christian faith, to the sacrifices of Sita and Ekalavya in Hindu mythology. He finds both traditions unreasonable and exploitative and invites humanity into a realm that rejects blind faith in favour of a reason-based scepticism of religious iconography.

FIKR

Khwabon ki basharat ki sadaqat mat puchh
Andhe ahkam ki andhi ye ita'at mat puchh
Qurban ho javaani eeman ke naam par
Bandhi jo ankh pe patti tha parda aql par
Dhobi ki baat dharm ka farmaan ban gayi
Sita ki baat vahm ka ilzam ban gayi
Chalne se aag par bhi na mushkil hui asaan
Neeti dharam ke naam pe Sita hui qurban

Yakta tha Eklavya bhi apne kamal mein
Phaansa is liye use jati ke jaal mein
Neeti dharam pe dhabba lagega ye dar jo tha
Kaata angotha ta kahen adna janam jo tha

Andhi neeti, andha imaan, ta'at bhi hai andhi
    kyoon
Khudgharzi ka jal banaya chhupi hui hai baat ye
    kyoon
Kab tak apni aql ko insaan band kivad mein rakkhega
Kab tak neet, dharam, eeman ko andha ban kar poojega
Neeti, rivaj, hukm-e khuda sab hi kya vajib ham par
In ki sazish bani siyasat aur jamaya hukum ham par
Neeti, rivaj, hukm-e Khuda sab ka bol bana mutlaq
Bol ke peechhe apna maqsad chhup ke kiya pura
    bahaq

Tod den is andhi ita'at ka tassalut
La-diniyat se hai hamein ye fikr ki davat
Vo fikr jo khoon-e javani ko yoon qurbaan na kare

Vo fikr jo andhe rivayat ki hami na bhare
Vo fikr jo mizaan mein dharam ko tole
Vo fikr jo har neeti kasauti pe kase
Vo fikr khudai ke jo farmaan jaanche
Vo fikr jo khwabon ki basharat se bache
Vo fikr jo tahqeeq ki koshish to kare
Vo fikr jo inkar ki jura'at bhi kare
Vo fikr jo ankh pe patti na bandhe, aql pe parda

THOUGHT

Ask not of the veracity of revealed dreams
Ask not of blind obeisance to blind orders
That youth be sacrificed at the altar of faith
The blindfold on the eyes, a curtain draped on the
        intellect.

A washerman's throwaway line launches a religious
        edict
And Sita is enveloped in a suspicious accusation
A walk across fire fails to prove her purity
Sita is sacrificed in the name of dharma.

Ekalavya, unique at the apex of his skill
But he too is ensnared in the web of caste
Fearful that tradition and faith might be stained
Is tricked to cut his own thumb, circumscribed by low
        birth.

Blind tradition, blind faith, why is obeisance blind
        too?
Why does the self-serving snare remain hidden?

How long will humans trap their intellect in locked
    rooms?
How long will they pray blindly to traditions?

All these traditions made compulsory by God's will
A conspiracy this, to rule over us
All these traditions made inevitable by God's will
Hidden is the motive that underlies them

Let us break this cycle of blind devotion
Impiety invites us into the realm of reason:
The thought that refuses to sacrifice youth
The thought that rejects blind folklore
The thought that puts religion on the scale
The thought that tests tradition on a touchstone
The thought that re-examines godly commands
The thought that sidesteps revealed dreams
The thought that at least attempts to question
The thought that even dares to refuse
The thought that neither blindfolds the eye nor
    curtails the intellect.

JAVED AKHTAR

After Sahir and Majrooh, the expression of the progressive aesthetic as well as the use of Urdu vocabulary in Hindi films is a responsibility that has been shouldered admirably by Javed Akhtar (b. 1945). Akhtar's film poetry has been close to the traditions established by his PWA predecessors, but he has maintained his poetic originality.

In 1995, Akhtar's book of poetry *Tarkash* hit the shelves, and became an instant hit in multiple languages. One hopes for similar success for his new book *Lava*, which was published in 2012. David Matthews has competently translated *Tarkash* into English in a well-laid-out book.[1] Akhtar's poetry is infused with a delectable use of Persian vocabulary—not many current lyricists would use *'posheeda'* (hidden) and *'khwabeeda'* (dreamy) in a movie song, as in a song from the 1998 movie *Wajood*. His lyrics ingeniously emphasize the common heritage of Hindi, Urdu and Hindustani. Take, for instance, how this purveyor of Persian words effortlessly and unselfconsciously inserts *khadi boli* and Sanskritized Hindi in the songs of the 2001 hit *Lagaan* (Tax): *'Bijuri ki talwaar nahin, boondon ke baan chalaao'* ('Not the sword of lightning, use the bow of raindrops') or the Ramleela imagery in the 2005 film *Swades* (My Country): *'Pal pal hai bhaari vo bipta hai aayi'* ('Each moment is weighty, such is my misfortune'). It is an interesting and welcome sidelight that, apart from being highly competent, Akhtar is a very 'conscious' lyricist, who not only pays attention to situations, tonalities, dialects and an overall narrative motive while writing his songs, but is very articulate in his ability to dissect and explain his choice of words and metre. Akhtar's personal website contains several video clips of him reciting his work.[2]

In an earlier book, Ali Mir and I have devoted a chapter to Akhtar's non-film poetry, and have also analysed his film songs.[3] In this volume, I translate three of his poems: '*Mother Teresa*', '*Aasaar-e Qadeema*' ('Ancient Remnants') and '*Ye Khel Kya Hai*' ('What Game Is This?'). The first two are from *Tarkash,* while the third is from *Lava.*

1   MOTHER TERESA

> *Ai ma Teresa*
> *Mujh ko teri azmat se inkar nahin hai*
> *Jaane kitne sookhe lab aur veeran aankhen*
> *Jaane kitne thhake badan aur zakhmi roohen*
> *Koodaghar mein roti ka ek tukda dhoondte nange*
>   *bachhe*
> *Footpathon par galte sadte buddhe kodi*
> *Jaane kitne beghar bedar bekas insan*
> *Jaane kitne toote kuchle bebas insan*
> *Teri chhaon mein jeene ki himmat paate hain*
> *Inko apne hone ki jo sazaa mili hai*
> *Us hone ki sazaa se thhodi si hi sahi, mohlat paate*
>   *hain*
> *Tera lams maseeha hai*
> *Aur tera karam hai ek samandar*
> *Jis ka koi paar nahin hai*

Ai ma Teresa
Mujh ko teri azmat se inkar nahin hai

Main thehra khudggarz
Bas ek apni hi khatir jeena wala
Main tujh se kis moonh se poochhoon
Tu ne kabhi ye kyon nahin poochhaa
Kis ne in bad-haalon ko bad-haal kiya hai?
Tu ne kabhi ye kyon nahin socha
Kaun si taaqat insanon ko footpathon aur
   koodagharon tak pahunchati hai
Tu ne kabhi ye kyon nahin dekha
Wahi nizam-e zar
Jis ne in bhookon se roti chheeni hai
Tere kahe par bhookon ke aage
Kuchh tukde daal raha hai
Tu ne kabhi ye kyon nahin chaaha
Nange bacche, buddhe kodi, bebas insaan
Is duniya se jeene ka haq maangen
Jeene ki khairaat na maange
Aisa kyon hai
Ik jaanib mazloom se tujh ko hamdardi hai
Doosri jaanib zaalim se bhi aar nahin hai?

Lekin sach hai
Aisi baaten main tujh se kis moonh se poochhoon?
Poochhoonga to mujh pe bhi vo zimmedari aa jaayegi
Jis se main bachta aaya hoon

Behtar hai, khamosh rahoon main
Aur agar kuchh kehna hai to yehi kahoon main
Ai ma Teresa
Mujh ko teri azmat se inkar nahin hai

MOTHER TERESA

O Mother Teresa
Your greatness, I am not one to deny
Wonder how many dry lips and desolate eyes
Wonder how many tired bodies and wounded souls
The naked children who root around garbage dumps
     seeking a piece of bread
Lepers rotting on pavements
Wonder how many homeless, rootless, hopeless people
Wonder how many broken, trampled, helpless people
Enter your hearth and find the courage to live
The punishment that is their existence
From that, they find respite, however fleeting
Your touch is a messiah
And your kindness an ocean
That is boundless
O Mother Teresa
Your greatness, I am not one to deny.

I am but a selfish person
Who lives only for himself
With what face can I ask you—
Why did you never ask
Who has rendered these pitiful people so pitiful?
Why did you never think
What power consigns human beings to lives on
    pavements and garbage dumps?
Why did you never see
That the same elite regime
That has stolen the food from these hungry mouths
Is, on your bidding,
Throwing a few scraps their way?

Why did you never wish
That these naked children, these old lepers, these
    helpless people
Demand from this world the right to live
Not the permission, the largesse to live?
Why is it so
On one hand you love the oppressed
But the oppressor too, you do not decry?

But it is true
With what face can I ask that of you?
If I did ask
The whole responsibility would become my task
Which, so far, I have chosen to avoid.

Better that I should hold my peace
And if I have to open my mouth, I should say please
O Mother Teresa
Your greatness, I am not one to deny.

2   AASAAR-E QADEEMA

Ek patthar ki adhuri moorat
Chand taambe ke puraane sikke
Kaali chaandi ke ajab se zevar
Aur kai kaanse ke toote bartan

Ek sehra mein mile zer-e zameen
Log kehte hain ke sadiyon pehle
Aaj sehra hai jahaan
Wahin ek shehr hua karta thha

Aur mujh ko ye khayaal aata hai
Kisi taqreeb, kisi mehfil mein
Saamna tujh se mera aaj bhi ho jaata hai
Ek lamhe ko, bas ik pal ke liye
Jism ki aanch, uchat-ti si nazar
Surkh bindiya ki damak
Sarsaraahat tere malboos ki, baalon ki mehak
Bekhayaali mei kabhi lams ka nanha sa phool

Aur phir door tak vahi sehra
Vahi sehra ke jahaan
Kabhi ik shehr hua karta thha

ANCIENT REMNANTS

A shattered stone statue, old copper coins
Strange ornaments of blackened silver
And several broken bronze vessels
Were found underground in a desert.

And people divined that centuries ago
A city had existed there.

And I remember
Seeing you by chance in a gathering, a party
For a moment, just for a second
The warmth of your body, your momentary gaze
The shine of red vermilion, the rustle of your clothes
The smell of your hair, and unconsciously, a tiny
        flower of touch

And again, that unending desert
That desert where once
There used to be a city.

3   YE KHEL KYA HAI

Mere mukhaalif ne chaal chal di hai
Aur ab
Meri chaal ke intezaar mein hai
Magar main kab se
Safed khaanon
Siyaah khaanon mein rakkhe
Kaale safed mohron ko dekhta hoon
Main sochta hoon
Ye mohre kya hain

Agar main samjhoon
Ki ye jo mohre hain
Sirf lakdi ke hain khilone
To jeetna kya hai haarna kya
Na ye zaroori
Na vo aham hai
Agar khushi hai na jeetne ki
Na haarne ka bhi koi gham hai
To khel kya hai
Main sochta hoon
Jo khelna hai
To apne dil mein yaqeen kar loon
Ye mohre sach-much ke baadshah-o-vazeer
Sach-much ke hain piyaade
Aur in ke aage hai
Dushmanon ki vo fauj

Rakhti hai jo mujh ko tabaah karne ke
Saare mansoobe
Sab iraade
Magar main aisa jo maan bhi loon
To sochta hoon
Ye khel kab hai
Ye jang hai jis ko jeetna hai
Ye jang hai jis mein sab hai jaayaz
Koi ye kehta hai jaise mujh se
Ye jang bhi hai
Ye khel bhi hai
Ye jang hai par khiladiyon ki
Ye khel hai jang ki tarah ka
Main sochta hoon
Jo khel hai
Is mein is tarah ka usool kyon hai
Ki koi mohra rahe ke jaaye
Magar jo hai baadshah
Us par kabhi koi aanch bhi na aaye
Vazeer hi ko hai bas ijaazat
Ke jis taraf bhi vo chaahe jaaye

Main sochta hoon
Jo khel hai
Is mein is tarah ke usool kyon hai
Piyaada jab apne ghar se nikle
Palat ke vaapas na aane paaye
Main sochta hoon
Agar yahi hai usool
To phir usool kya hai
Agar yahi hai ye khel
To phir ye khel kya hai
Main in savaalon se jaane kab se ulajh raha hoon

Mere mukhalif ne chaal chal di hai
Aur ab meri chaal ke intezaar mein hai

WHAT GAME IS THIS?

My opponent has made a move
And now
Awaits mine.
But for ages
I stare at the black and white pieces
That lie on white and black squares
And I think
What are these pieces?

Were I to assume
That these pieces
Are no more than wooden toys
Then what is a victory or a loss?
If in winning there are no joys
Nor sorrows in losing
What is the game?
I think
If I must indeed play
Then I must believe
That these pieces are indeed king and minister
Indeed these are foot soldiers
And arrayed before them
Is that enemy army
Which harbours all plans evil
All schemes sinister
To destroy me
But were I to believe this

Then is this a game any longer?
This is a war that must be won
A war in which all is fair
It is as if somebody explains:
This is a war
And a game as well
It is a war, but between players
A game between warriors
I think
If it is a game
Then why does it have a rule
That whether a foot soldier stays or goes
The one who is king
Must always be protected?
That only the minister has the freedom
To move any which way?

I think
Why does this game
Have a rule
That once a foot soldier leaves home
He can never return?
I think
If this is the rule
Then what is a rule[4]?
If this is the game
Then what is the name of the game[5]?
I have been wrestling for ages with these questions
But my opponent has made a move
And awaits mine.

FAHMIDA RIAZ

It delighted my parochial heart to find that Fahmida Riaz
(b. 1946) had spent some childhood time in Hyderabad
before migrating to Pakistan. Her first book was published
at the precociously young age of twenty-two. Called *Patthar
ki Zaban* (The Language of Stones), it launched her as
a voice to be reckoned with in Urdu poetry. Her second
volume *Badan Dareeda* (The Body, Exposed) led to conservative
outcry, but provided a completely new idiom to Urdu
poetry. It was her outspoken political views that forced her to
go into exile; she lived in India, but has since returned to
Pakistan.[1]

My favourite translation of a Riaz poem, other than her
own efforts, is of '*Chadar aur Chaardiwaari*' ('The Veil and
the Four Walls of Home'), translated by my brother Ali Mir.[2]
In this anthology, I include three small poems/excerpts. The
first expressed her disillusionment at the Indian nuclear blasts
of 1998, comparing the silliness of that decision to that of her
own country's. The second is a stunningly evocative poem on
the practice of stoning adulterers, and is inspired by a historical
account of a stoning in which, while a couple was being stoned
to death, the man kept trying to shield his doomed lover from
the stones that would eventually take both their lives. The final
poem—a franker expression of female sexuality—refers to the
Biblical/Islamic tale in which Cain slew Abel when his sacrifice

of a goat was not accepted by Allah. In some versions, Cain had desired his sister Aqleema for himself although she was forbidden to him.

1   NAYA BHARAT

> *Tum bilkul hum jaise nikle*
> *Woh moorakhta, woh ghaamadpan*
> *Aakhir pahunchi dwaar tumhaare*
>
> *Prait dharam ka naach raha hai*
> *Saare ulte kaarya karoge*
> *Tum bhi baithe karoge socha*
> *Kaun hai Hindu, kaun nahin hai*
> *Ek jaap sa karte jao*
> *Kitna veer mahaan tha Bharat*

NEW INDIA

> You turned out just like us
> The same silliness, the same obstinacy
> Has finally reached your doorstep as well.
>
> Now that the mad ghost of religion has begun to
>   dance
> You will do everything wrong
> You will ask—Who is a true Hindu? Who is not?
> Now go and start chanting
> How great, how glorious was Bharat once!

2   **RAJM**

> *Paagal tan mein kyon basti hai*
> *Ye vahshi tareek aarzoo*
> *Bahut qadeem, udaas aarzoo*
> *Taareeki mein chhup jaane ki*
> *Ek lamhe ko*
> *Ek lamhe ko*
>
> *Rab-e Qahhar! Ye mojiza kya hai?*
> *Tera khalq kiya hua Aadam*
> *Lazzat-e sang ka kyon khwaahaan hai?*
> *Is ki sahr-zada cheekhon mein*
> *Ye kis barzakh ka naghma hai?*
> *Kya thhi badan ke zakhm ki lazzat?*
> *Betaabi se yoon raqsaan hai*
> *Har bun-e moonh se surkh-o-siyaah lahu ka darya*
>   *ubal pada hai*

STONING

> In the mad heart does reside
> A wild, dark desire
> An ancient desire, ineffably sad
> To be one with the blackness
> For a moment
> A moment.
>
> My overpowering God! What is this miracle
> That your creation, this Adam
> Seeks the pleasures of this mortal stoning?
> In which limbo was this song born?
> Why did the body seek these wounds?

It is as if it dances, impatient
While every wound froths with red and black blood.

3   AQLEEMA

Aqleema
Jo Habeel aur Qabeel ki maajaai hai
Maajaai
Magar mukhtalif
Mukhtalif beech mein raanon ke
Aur pistaanon ki ubhaar mein
Aur apne pet ke andar
Aur kookh mein
In sab ki qismat kyon hai
Ik farba bhed ke bachhe ki qurbani
Vo apne badan ki qaidi
Tapti hui dhoop mein jalte
Teeley par khadi hui hai
Patthar par naqsh bani hai
Is naqsh ko ghaur se dekho
Lambi raanon se oopar
Ubharte pistaano se oopar
Pecheeda kookh se oopar
Aqleema ka sar bhi hai
Allah, kabhi Aqleema bhi kalaam kare
Aur kuchh poochhe

AQLEEMA

Aqleema
Who was the sister of Abel and Cain

Sister
But different
Different between her thighs
And in the swell of her breasts
And inside her stomach
And in her womb
And the fate of all these body parts
Was linked to the sacrifice of a fattened goat.
She, a prisoner of her body,
Stands on a hillock
And burns in the hot sun
As if she has been drawn on stone
Look at this drawing carefully
Move above the long thighs
And the swell of the breasts
And above the complicated womb—
There is Aqleema's head
Allah, talk to Aqleema sometimes
Ask her something.

PARVEEN SHAKIR

Vo to khushboo hai, hawaaon mein bikhar jaayega
Mas'ala phool ka hai, phool kidhar jaayega

He is fragrance, and into the winds he will flow
The problem lies with the flower, where will it go?

Parveen Shakir (1952–94) was a civil servant in Pakistan,
who enjoyed immense fame before her untimely death in an
automobile accident. Her first book of poems, *Khushboo*, was
published when she was twenty-four.[1] Her use of feminine tropes
in the ghazal tradition marked her as an innovator in the form;
for example, she is considered a pioneer in the deployment of the
term '*khushboo*' (fragrance), or in referring to the protagonist
of the ghazal as '*ladki*' (girl). Her poetry was self-conscious in
rebelling against patriarchy. For example, consider the following
verse:

Aks-e khushboo hoon, bikharne se na roke koi
Aur bikhar jaaoon to mujh ko na samete koi

I am fragrance, nobody stop me from diffusing
And if I diffuse, nobody try to corral me.

Despite these obvious female-centric tropes, her poetry was still written mostly in the classical mode, and did not seem to aspire to the more consciously feminist aesthetic that her contemporaries in Pakistan like Kishwar Naheed, Fahmida Riaz, Ishrat Afreen and others pioneered. The ghazal I have chosen to translate here reflects this.[2]

KUCHH TO HAVA BHI SARD THHI

Kuchh to hava bhi sard thhi kuchh thha tera khayaal bhi
Dil ko khushi ke saath saath hota rahaa malaal bhi

Baat vo aadhi raat ki raat vo poore chaand ki
Chaand bhi ain chait kaa us pe teraa jamaal bhi

Sab se nazar bachaa ke vo mujh ko aise dekhta
Ek dafaa to ruk gayi gardish-e maah-o-saal bhi

Dil to chamak sakega kya phir bhi tarash ke dekh lo
Sheeshaa-garaan-e shahr ke haath ka ye kamaal bhi

Us ko na paa sake the jab dil ka ajeeb haal tha
Ab jo palat ke dekhiye baat thi kuchh muhaal bhi

Meri talab tha ek shakhs vo jo nahin milaa to phir
Haath dua se yoon gira bhool gaya savaal bhi

Shaam ki na'samajh hava, poochh rahi hai ek pata
Mauj-e hava-e koo-e yaar kuchh to meraa khayaal bhi

Us ke hi baazuon mein aur us ko hi sochte rahe
Jism ki khwaahishon pe thhe rooh ke aur jaal bhi

PARTLY THE BREEZE WAS COLD

Partly it was that the breeze was cold
And partly that I was thinking of you
Slowly that night, as my happiness grew
I felt a sharp twinge of that hurt old.

Let us talk then of that late night
That moment illuminated in the moon
The best of months, the moon of June
Illuminating your beauty in its light

Secretly, my love fixed me with his glance
While affecting a casual, insouciant air
It did seem once for a moment there
Time had stopped; the earth had ceased its dance.

How can you make a sad thing shine
But try you must to do your part
Can you brighten my broken heart
Dear jewellers of this city of mine?

My heart's sadness I could not quell
When I realized I'd never win him
But now that I reflect on my whim
The quest was quite impossible.

There was only one for whom I did care
When I could not have him, it transpired
That my hands at my sides stayed fixed, mired
No longer could I lift them in prayer.

The evening zephyr, so naive,
Seeks its destination till the end
Dear breeze of the street of my friend
Have some consideration for me.

In his embrace I did lay quiet
And all I did was think of him
Dominating my body's whim
My soul was a spiderweb, tight.

JAMEELA NISHAT

Jameela Nishat (b. 1955) was born in the old city of Hyderabad, and still lives and works there. She runs a resource centre for women, while fulfilling other commitments. An English teacher by training and profession, she imbues her poetry with a frank description of what it means to be a Muslim woman in a world where the twin forces of patriarchy and Islamophobia are ascendant.

Nishat's poetry was featured in the influential volume *Women Writing in India* (edited by Susie Tharu and K. Lalita). Her language is often infused with the idiom of her native Dakkani. The poem below speaks of the experience of Muslim women whose clothing leads them to be identified racially, almost as if it were an extension of their bodies, their selves. The poem hinges on a young Muslim girl who is driven away from the cinema hall by a *danda* (stick). This refers perhaps to the moral police that tries to prevent devout women from watching movies.

BURQA

Burqa pehan kar nikli
Degree bhi main ne li
Computers main ne seekha
Doosron se aage

265

Main ne khud ko paaya
Ammi bhi bahut khush thhi
Abba bhi bahut khush
Haathon mein apne
Main ne
Koh-e Toor uthaya
Zamaane ko raund daloon
Ye dil mein main ne thhana
Ban jaaoongi Sikandar
Kali naqaab ke andar
Har saans ne pukaara

Mauj masti main karne nikli
Theatre mein joonhi pahunchi
Dande ne mujh ko roka
Burqa mana hai ladki
Kaale naqaab mein kaala dhuaan sa uthha
Us waqt
Vahin par
Main ne
Burqa utaar phenka

BURQA

I stepped out in a burqa
And yet graduated from college
Learned computer programming
And found myself
Head and shoulders ahead of my peers
My mother was thrilled
And my father, he was ecstatic
In my hands,

I held Mount Sinai
I could conquer this world
So my heart believed
I would be Alexander in a black veil
Every breath screamed.

One day I stepped out to have fun
And as I entered a cinema hall
Was accosted by a stick
'Girl, no burqas allowed here!'
From under the black veil arose the black smoke of
    fury
At that very moment
I
Threw away my burqa.

ISHRAT AFREEN

Ishrat Afreen (b. 1956) moved from Pakistan to India and then to the USA, and currently teaches at the University of Texas. She has her own official website[1], and has been publishing her poems since she was fifteen. Two of her collections have been published, one in the 1980s and one, more recently, in 2005: *Dhoop Apne Hisse Ki* (My Share of Sunlight). One can watch her perform her poetry in the public domain. Her poems published in Rukhsana Ahmed's anthology, *Beyond Belief: Contemporary Feminist Urdu Poetry* (1990), deployed a rawness that consciously gendered the poetic experience.[2]

Here, I include two poems. The first is one of my favourites for its 'take-no-prisoners' attitude and its direct evocativeness. The second poem positions her more in the tradition of the progressive writers, especially Makhdoom, who sought to see beauty in labour and valued women's labour through traditional invocations of beauty. Afreen takes the metaphors much further, though, positioning them directly against the ephemeral concept of beauty associated with privilege.

1   INTESAAB

> *Mera qad*
> *Mere baap se ooncha nikla*
> *Aur meri maa jeet gayi*

DEDICATION

I grew taller than my father.
My mother had won.

2   **GULAAB AUR KAPAAS**

Kheton mein kaam karti hui ladkiyaan
Jeth ki champai dhoop ne
Jin ka sona badan
Surmayi kar diya
Jin ko raaton mein os aur paale kaa bistar mile
Din ko sooraj saron par jale

Ye hare lawn mein
Sang-e marmar ke benchon pe baithi hui
Un haseen mooraton se kahin khoobsoorat
Kahin mukhtalif
Jin ke joode mein joohi ki kaliyan sajee
Jo gulaab aur bele ki khushboo liye
Aur rangon ki hiddat se paagal phiren

Khet mein dhoop chunti hui ladkiyaan bhi
Nai umr ki sabz dehleez par hain magar
Aaina tak nahin dekhteen
Ye gulaab aur dezi ki hiddat se naa-aashna
Khushboo-on ke javan-lams se bekhabar
Phool chunti hain lekin pahanti nahin
In ke malboos mein
Tez sarson ke phoolon ki baas
Un ki aankhon mein roshan kapaas

ROSES AND COTTON

These girls who toil in the fields
Whose golden skin has been dyed dark by the sun
Who sleep on beds of frost and dew at night
And are burned by the sun in the day.

They are much prettier than those statues
Sitting on marble benches
On green lawns
Prettier and more different
Than those whose tresses are adorned with roses and
    jasmine buds
And who run wild in a sharp profusion of colours.

The girls who pluck sunlight in the farms
Are also at the green threshold of the new era, but
Do not even look at mirrors
They are unfamiliar with the sharpness of rose and
    juhi
They pluck the flowers, but do not wear them
Their clothes carry the pungent scent
Of mustard flowers instead
And their eyes the brightness of cotton.

ZEESHAN SAHIL

Zeeshan Sahil (1961–2008) was an accomplished poet whose untimely demise deprived Urdu of a remarkable voice. I include him here as a representative of the 'caged beasts'—seven remarkable new voices that were introduced to English-speaking readers in a 1999 book titled *An Evening of Caged Beasts: Seven Postmodernist Urdu Poets*[1]. His poems on the city of Karachi were remarkable in their use of rhythms of children playing to invoke the city's resilience and terror, even as it attempted to preserve its own sanity in an era when lawlessness was the order of the day. In his own words:

> It is a lie that in Karachi, after the rain, the sprouting grass doesn't have blades deep green and soft. Or that the trees do not give shade without the help of clouds . . . With us in Karachi live birds who fly from trees through the sound of bullets and bombs; perch on walls; always they gather somewhere to pray. Our books don't wait inside cupboards for termites. Now our hearts swim these seas where once our eyes searched for golden flowers and our hands tear down the walls that once buried us alive.[2]

The first short poem I have translated below reflects Sahil's ability to show (with such economy of language) how categories

271

are the product of human thought. The poem turns around the poetic rhyme of '*rasta*' (path) and '*basta*' (the wanderer's bag), and the idea of forgetful humans, wandering without realizing that they have the moon and the stars in their bags. The second poem beautifully invokes the joy of the quotidian: how a mere bus journey with a friend or the memory of a lover's modest room can be the basis of joy and reflection, and how memory imposes itself on the consciousness through minor, slight observations.

1   **NAZM**

> *Zindagi adhoori hai*
> *Lekin us mein har lamha*
> *Khwaab aur mohabbat ki*
> *Aarzoo zaroori hai*
> *Khwaab aur mohabbat hi*
> *Aadmi ke chalne ko raaste banaate hain*
> *Chaand aur sitaaron ko*
> *Aaasmaan se laakar*
> *Zindagi ke raste mein*
> *Aadmi ke baste mein*
> *Rakh ke bhool jaate hain*

POEM

> Life is incomplete
> But in it, every moment
> Needs the desire
> Brought by dreams and love
> For it is dreams and love
> That transform human wandering

Into ordered paths
And bring the moon and the stars
From the skies
To the path that life takes
Into the rucksacks that humans carry around
Who having placed them there
Forget about them.

2 TUMHAARE LIYE EK NAZM

Hamesha rehne ke liye
Ye duniya kitni na-munasib jagah hai
Aur zindagi har roz
Pehle se ziyaada na qaabil-e bardaasht
Lekin Saiduddin ke saath
Bus mein safar karne waali khushi
Aur tumhaare dressing table par
Jalne waali batti se behta hua mom
Aur aaine par jamne waala dhuaan
Har cheez ki jagah le lete hain
Meri kitaabon mein band phool
Khwaabon ke jangal ban jaate hain
Tum Formica par jami gard pe
Apni ungliyon se bahut se
Raaste banaati ho
Beshumaar khaali raaston waale shahr mein
Raat gehri hone par tumhaari
Door-uftaada maujoodgi
Sitaaron ko ghair-zaroori, chaand ko faaltu
Aur samandar ko izaafi cheez banaa deti hain
Tumhaari yaad, aur apne dil par
Badhte hue dabaao se ghabraa kar

Main dua maangta hoon
Shaayaron se khuda ki musalsal naaraazgi
Ke baavujood meri dua
Hamesha tum se shuroo hoti hai

A POEM FOR YOU

As a place to stay in continually
This world is so undesirable
And life, every day,
Becomes ever more unbearable.
But some pleasures abound.
The journey on the bus with Saiduddin
And that congealed wax on your dressing table
From the worn-down candle
And the residue of smoke on your mirror
Take the place of all else.
The pressed flowers in my books
Become the deep forests of dreams.
You draw many paths with your fingers
On the dust that settles on the Formica
And when night settles on that city of countless empty
      paths
Your distant presence makes stars unnecessary, the
      moon useless
And turns the sea into something redundant.
Your memory and the heaviness in my heart scare me
And I begin to pray.
Despite God's unceasing anger toward poets
My prayer always begins with you.

NOTES

Foreword

1. When I approached Gulzar Saheb to write a foreword, he was kind enough to suggest that he write it as a poem, and I obviously accepted that idea gratefully. I enclose the Urdu version of his introductory paragraph here: '*Urdu zaban apne aap mein ek riyasat hai. Vo jahaan jaati hai, apni zameen bana leti hai. Hindustan mein paida hui, magar sirf Hindustan ki nahin. Pakistan ki sarkari zaban hai. Lekin sirf Pakistan ki nahin. Oslo (Norway) gayi to vahaan bas gayi. Bartaniya gayi to vahaan bhi apni jagah bala li. Canada gayi to ek aur basti bas gayi. Amreeka gayi to vahaan ki ho gayi. Raza Mir ne god le liya.*

   '*Sach to ye hai ke agar "god lena" ki jagah aisa koi muhaavra hota to kahte: "labon pe le liya." Jahaan jaati hai, seene se lag jaati hai. Vo rivayat ho jaati hai. Dastoor ho jaati hai. Urdu ek tehzeeb ki awaaz hai.*'

Preface

1. My teachers over time have included such stalwarts as Amar Dehlavi (who published the Amar Publications chapbooks of Urdu poets); K.C. Kanda (whose translations of Urdu ghazals and nazms are veritable labours of love); Nita Awatramani's Urdu Poetry Archive (www.urdupoetry.com); older bulletin boards like rec. music.indian.misc and alt.language.urdu.poetry (both of which

are now Google groups); Victor G. Kiernan's translations of Faiz and Iqbal—*Poems by Faiz* (London: George Allen and Unwin, 1971) and *Poems from Iqbal* (Karachi: Oxford University Press, 1999); Khushwant Singh's translations of Rajinder Singh Bedi [*I Take This Woman* (Delhi: Penguin India, 1994)], Iqbal [*Shikwa and Jawab-i-Shikwa: Iqbal's Dialogue with Allah* (Delhi: Oxford University Press, 1997)] and Mirza Hadi Ruswa [*The Courtesan of Lucknow: Umrao Jan Ada*, translated by Khushwant Singh and M.A. Husaini (New Delhi: Orient Paperbacks, 1961)]; Frances W. Pritchett's awesome website http://www.columbia.edu/~fp7 that includes translations of the *Deevan-e Ghalib* as well as Mir's ghazals; C.M. Naim and M.U. Memon's editorship of the *Annual of Urdu Studies* (http://urdustudies.com/); Mehr Afshan Farooqi's two-volume history of Urdu literature—*The Oxford India Anthology of Modern Urdu Literature*, 2 vols (New Delhi: Oxford University Press, 2008); and numerous others. A recent site that I would recommend highly is www.urdushahkar.org, which is maintained by S.M. Shahed, and which provides accessible translations for a variety (and increasing corpus) of poems, and includes transliteration, Urdu script versions, and audio files with performance and exegesis.

Introduction: The Flutter of Angel Wings

1. Refers to the debt incurred by anyone who eats salt in another's home.
2. Dilip Kumar's wonderful rendition of this poem is available as a video in the public domain on YouTube.
3. *Na ho jab* = if there is no; *phir* = then; *kyon* = why; *yaqeenan* = certainly; *milawat* = adulteration; *shab ko* = to the night.
4. In the interests of full disclosure, I am a great partisan of the Progressive Writers' Association, and believe that the best poetry in Urdu was produced during the progressive phase. I have co-authored with Ali Husain Mir a book on the topic titled *Anthems of Resistance: A Celebration of Progressive Urdu Poetry* (New

Delhi: Roli Books, 2006).

5. I have dealt extensively with this phenomenon elsewhere: '"Voh Yar Hai jo Khusbu ki Tarah / Jis ki Zuban Urdu ki Tarah": The Friendly Association Between Urdu Poetry and Hindi Film Music,' *Annual of Urdu Studies* 15 (2000), http://www.urdustudies.com/pdf/15/18mir.pdf.

6. See Akbar Hyder, 'Urdu's Progressive Wit: Sulaiman Khatib, Sarvar "Danda" and the Subaltern Satirists Who Spoke Up,' *Annual of Urdu Studies* 20 (2005), http://www.urdustudies.com/pdf/20/07AkbarHyder.pdf.

7. Online portals have proved to be a treasure trove of the work of these poets, and I would urge you to seek out the performances of some of their verses on sites like YouTube.

8. Those wishing to start reading right away on this issue may consider starting with Carla Petievich's essay 'Feminine Authorship and Urdu Poetic Tradition: Baharistan-i Naz vs. Tazkira-i Rekhti,' in *A Wilderness of Possibilities: Urdu Studies in Transnational Perspective*, edited by Kathryn Hansen and David Lelyveld (New Delhi: Oxford University Press, 2005). Also see Gail Minault's 'Other Voices, Other Rooms: The View from the Zenana,' in *Women as Subjects*, edited by Nita Kumar (Calcutta: Stree, 1994); and Ruth Vanita's *Gender, Sex, and the City: Urdu Rekhti Poetry in India, 1780–1870* (New York: Macmillan, 2012). Minault's essay—'Begamati Zuban: Women's Language and Culture in Nineteenth-Century Delhi,' in *India International Centre Quarterly* 11, no. 2 (1984): 155–70—is also instructive. An Urdu article from the 1930s, Nasiruddin Hashmi's 'Khavatin-e Dakkan ki Urdu khidmaat,' *Sabras* 1, no. 1: 120–24, mentions three thirteenth-century women poets of Hyderabad, named Chanda Bai, Sharfunnisa and Fatima, who may be available in print—I'm on the prowl . . .

9. The four-volume set was produced bilingually and titled *Vazahat-e Urdu Kitabiyat (Imrani Uloom)* in Urdu, and *Annotated Urdu Bibliography (Social Sciences)* in English. Both were published by the Educational Publishing House in New Delhi in 2008.

Amir Khusrau

1. My selection unfortunately throws his more serious work in the shadows, but the Khusrau enthusiast may find a lot more joy at 'Amir Khusrau Website,' compiled by Yousuf Saeed, http://www.angelfire.com/sd/urdumedia/index.html.

Quli Qutub Shah

1. For more on Quli Qutub Shah, see Narendra Luther's appreciative essay, 'A Multi-faceted Prince,' Narendra Luther Archives, http://narendralutherarchives.blogspot.com/2006/12/multi-faceted-prince.html.

Mirza Sauda

1. This verse has been beautifully performed by singers like Ustad Salamat Ali Khan and Tina Sani. Recordings of both these performances are available on YouTube.

Khwaja Mir Dard

1. The interested reader who wishes to follow up on Dard will find a lot in Ian Bedford's paper on the difficulties of translating from Dard's eighteenth-century Urdu idiom into English, which includes a competent translation of twelve of his best-known ghazals: 'Approaching Khvaja Mir Dard,' *Annual of Urdu Studies* 22 (2007), http://www.urdustudies.com/pdf/22/04IanBedford.pdf; or in Homayra Ziad's essay, 'The Nature and Art of Discourse in the Religious Writings of Khvaja Mir Dard,' *Annual of Urdu Studies* 20 (2005), http://www.urdustudies.com/pdf/20/10Ziad.pdf. Both commentators seem to agree that Dard's spiritual (Sufi) leanings influenced his poetry greatly.

Mir Taqi Mir

1. While one could dedicate several books to Mir's work, the true enthusiast is directed to the page maintained most painstakingly by

F.W. Pritchett, 'A Garden of Kashmir,' Columbia University, http://www.columbia.edu/itc/mealac/pritchett/00garden/index.html; as well as to C.M. Naim's translation of Mir's autobiography, which is itself a marvel of literary merit and an extraordinary exposition of a chequered life—C.M. Naim, *Zikr-i Mir: The Autobiography of the Eighteenth Century Mughal Poet: Mir Muhammad Taqi 'Mir' (1723–1810)* (New Delhi: Oxford University Press, 1999), excerpts from which are published in 'Mir on His Patrons,' *Annual of Urdu Studies* 14 (1999), http://www.urdustudies.com/pdf/14/08naimcMiron.pdf, along with Naim's analysis in 'Mir and His Patrons,' *Annual of Urdu Studies* 14 (1999), http://www.urdustudies.com/pdf/14/07naimcMirand.pdf.

2. For example, this verse shows his love for a young man: '*Mir kya saade hain, beemar hue jis ke sabab, Usi attar ke bete se dawaa lete hain*' ('Mir is so simple-minded, he seeks medicine from the very apothecary's son, who has caused him to fall ill').

3. Of its many renditions in the public domain, I like the one by Nusrat Fateh Ali Khan a lot, but recommend the one by Shishir Parkhie even more strongly. Both versions are available on YouTube.

Insha

1. See Christopher Shackle and Rupert Snell's exposition of the poem and their discussion of Insha's life at 'Insha Allah Khan, *Rani Ketki ki Kahani* (c. 1803),' Columbia University, http://www.columbia.edu/itc/mealac/pritchett/00urduhindilinks/shacklesnell/302insha.pdf.

Mir Anees

1. The interested reader may find much more about Anees at 'Mir Anees: A Poet Extraordinaire,' edited by Abu Talib Rizvi, http://www.miranees.com/. A longer marsiya has been translated by David Matthews, and is available in the public domain at http://razarumi.com/?p=794.

Bahadur Shah Zafar

1. Those who are interested in the poet-king would do well to visit 'Bahadur Shah Zafar,' http://www.kapadia.com/zafar.html—a website that contains a trove of information about him, including history, poetry and even a photograph (the sole photograph of a Mughal emperor!).

Zauq

1. In order to access the deevan electronically, see Malik-ul Shaura, Khaqani-e Hind and Shaikh Ibrahim Zauoq, 'Deewan-e Zauq,' Allama Iqbal Urdu Cyber Library, http://www.urducl.com/Urdu-Books/969-416-207-003/.

2. See Mohammad Husain Azad, *Aab-e Hayaat: Shaping the Canon of Urdu Poetry*, translated and edited by F.W. Pritchett and Shamsur Rahman Faruqi (New Delhi: Oxford University Press, 2001).

3. In particular, I'd recommend Begum Akhtar's rendition of *'Laayi hayaat aaye'* and Jagjit Singh's version of *'Ab to ghabraa ke'*, both of which are available on YouTube.

4. The prophet Khizr is known to have lived for an inordinately long time.

Mirza Ghalib

1. For some interesting commentary, see F.W. Pritchett, '"The Meaning of the Meaningless Verses": Ghalib and his Commentators,' in *A Wilderness of Possibilities*, 251–72; it can be read at http://www.columbia.edu/itc/mealac/pritchett/00fwp/published/ghalib_commentary2.pdf. Pritchett marshals a variety of expositions of this sher from multiple *sharah*s and commentaries, and rightly concludes that the search for definitive meanings in poetry is simultaneously futile, arrogant and reductive.

2. Other places to look for Ghalibiana on the Internet include Pritchett's work on Ghalib's deevan (available on the web at 'A Desertful of Roses: The Urdu Ghazals of Mirza Asadullah Khan

"Ghalib",' F.W. Pritchett and Columbia University, http://www.columbia.edu/itc/mealac/pritchett/00ghalib/index.html); and 'Wine of Passion: The Urdu Ghazals of Ghalib,' http://ghalib.org/, maintained by Dr Sarfaraz Niazi.

3. I would recommend Jagjit Singh's rendition of '*Aah ko chahiye*'. Mohammad Rafi does a great job of rendering '*Bas ke dushwaar*' in his trademark clean style, and also does justice to '*Bazeecha-e atfaal*'. Begum Akhtar sings '*Sab kahaan kuchh*' in breathtaking fashion (the version I heard at http://www.youtube.com/watch?v=qqp_27apaVA included a bonus reading of a snippet from one of Ghalib's letters in Kaifi Azmi's dreamy voice). I would recommend a return to Jagjit Singh for '*Hazaaron khwaahishein*'.

4. This refers to a folk reference that some raindrops, when they fall into the sea, are swallowed by oysters and become pearls. It is a metaphor for the difficulties that are encountered in the journey toward fulfilment.

5. For Muslims, the sign of the new moon announces the festival, and here, Ghalib connects the curve of the executioner's scimitar to the curve of the moon, to describe a martyr's passion.

6. Ghalib is being ironical here.

7. Lovers eventually find their clothes torn or bloodstained.

8. Agha Shahid Ali translated this ghazal rhythmically; it can be read at 'Agha Shahid Ali: "Not All, Only A Few Return" (After Ghalib),' golempoem, http://matthewsalomon.wordpress.com/2007/12/28/agha-shahid-ali-not-all-only-a-few-return-after-ghalib/.

9. Perhaps Ghalib is extolling nightlife here. The constellation referred to is the *Banatunnash* (literally, 'the daughters of the bier', a name for the constellation Ursa Major, usually associated in Urdu poetry with beautiful women).

10. The poet's feelings provided the material for the nightingale's songs, so he thinks of himself as a teacher here.

11. Why would you want to be the scribe to letters written by your lover? Curiosity, jealousy, or a Cyrano de Bergerac–style attempt to communicate your own feelings through other suitors? You be the judge. In this day and age, Ghalib may have written verses about peeking into his lover's Facebook page!

12. Referring to one's love as infidel is an old practice in the ghazal tradition; it indicates that, at its peak, love begins to resemble worship, and so produces religiously undesirable effects.

13. Over the course of time, Ghalib's poetry has occasionally been infiltrated, sometimes by people who deleted a few verses, and at others by those who inserted a few 'rogue verses' in it. Purists swear that this is one such rogue verse that Ghalib never wrote. This, however, is not a book for purists, and I also include it to highlight this delightful phenomenon of plagiarism-in-reverse.

14. Ghalib at his best. Without my parenthetic comments, the words sound cryptic. But once illuminated, the sher shows myriad possibilities. For example, what does it mean to say that a desert is hidden by dust? Ghalib deploys the metaphor of 'being left in the dust' to indicate an upstaging. The desolation of the poet shames the dryness of the desert, just as his tears upstage the oceans in their volume.

15. This is the recrimination of the dumped lover, who accuses the beloved (who is presumably either pale or red-faced, you decide).

16. The poet, at death's door, seeks to remain close to his killer libations. You may choose to read this as a denunciation of habit, or a celebration of faithfulness, or . . . knock yourself out!

Momin

1. A very good rendition of this ghazal can be found in the 1981 film *Kudrat*. I would also urge you to listen to Begum Akhtar's beautiful rendition. Both can be found on YouTube.

Dagh Dehlavi

1. Some of his poems with English translations can be read at 'Daagh Dehlvi: Famous Poet at Allpoetry,' Kevin, http://allpoetry.com/Daagh_Dehlvi.

2. '*Lutf voh*' was performed by Noorjehan and is available on YouTube. While '*Sabaq aisa*' was set to music by A.R. Rahman for the 2003 film *Tehzeeb*, and sung evocatively by Madhushree, my favourite is Shruti Shadolikar's composition, set to Raag Kaafi (in Dadra Taal, for the cognoscenti), which is, again, available on YouTube.

Mohammed Iqbal

1. See Muhammad Suheyl Umar, 'Iqbal—Poet-Philosopher,' Iqbal Academy Pakistan, http://allamaiqbal.com/.
2. See Kiernan, *Poems from Iqbal*.
3. The poem first appeared in Iqbal's *Baal-i Gibreel* (Gabriel's Wing) in 1935. For a translation and discussion of that poem, see Varis Alavi, 'Gabriel and Lucifer,' *Annual of Urdu Studies* 20 (2005), http://www.urdustudies.com/pdf/20/04Alavi Lucifer.pdf.
4. Iqbal here references the love between Mahmud of Ghazni and his slave Ayaz. This is a metaphor for the ideal love that breaks all boundaries of class and status (and, incidentally, decentres heterosexual normativity).

Brij Narain Chakbast

1. These poems have been well analysed by Neil Krishan Aggarwal in 'The Rama Story of Brij Narain Chakbast,' *Annual of Urdu Studies* 22 (2007), http://www.urdustudies.com/pdf/22/11AggarwalChakbast.pdf.
2. This is an excerpt from the eponymous poem.

Jigar Moradabadi

1. I have used the male and female pronouns in consecutive shers to highlight that there is no default gender in many ghazals. Indeed, more often than not, the object of the poet's affection is male.

Firaaq Gorakhpuri

1. For elaboration, see Ruth Vanita and Salim Kidwai, *Same Sex Love in India: Readings from History and Literature* (New Delhi: Penguin Books India, 2008), 264–66.

Josh Malihabadi

1. Refers to the 1757 Battle of Plassey, in which Robert Clive defeated Nawab Sirajuddowlah, through the connivance of his general, Mir Jafar.
2. Bahadur Shah Zafar's two sons were beheaded and their heads sent to him as a punishment for his role in the 1857 war. Zafar died in Rangoon, which is referred to later in the poem.
3. Metiaburj was where Wajid Ali Shah, the king of Avadh, was imprisoned; he died and was buried in Qaisar Bagh, nearby. Wajid Ali Shah's takhallus was Akhtar, which is referred to in the poem.
4. Josh may not be referring to Reginald Dyer, who perpetrated the Jalianwala Bagh massacre (he died in 1927) but to Michael O'Dwyer, the lieutenant governor of Punjab in the JB massacre days, who supported Dyer's actions, and was alive then (he was assassinated by Udham Singh in 1940).
5. In Islamic history, Husain is the ultimate symbol of the righteous person who suffered injustice; Yazid and Shimr are the paradigmatic dispensers of tyranny and injustice.

Makhdoom Mohiuddin

1. Of the many renditions of this poem, the best perhaps is the version sung by Jagjit Singh and Asha Bhonsle, which is available on YouTube.

Majaz

1. A rendition of the whole poem in Majaz's own voice can be found on YouTube.

2. This is an excerpt from the eponymous poem.
3. Chengiz Khan and Nadir Shah are notorious in Indian history as raiders and despoilers of local wealth.
4. A gathering of kings in Hindu mythology. Serves here as a metaphor for an assembly of the elite.

N.M. Rashid

1. For an analysis of one of his poems titled '*Samandar ki Tah mein*' ('Under the Sea'), see Muhammad Hasan Askari's piece 'A Poem by Rashid: An Analysis,' *Annual of Urdu Studies* 24 (2009), http://www.urdustudies.com/pdf/24/10AskariRashid.pdf. Rashid's friend Miraji analysed two of his poems, translations of which can be found in 'Two Poems by Rashid: An Analytical Reading,' by Riyaz Latif in *Annual of Urdu Studies* 24 (2009), http://www.urdustudies.com/pdf/24/11MirajiRashid.pdf.

Faiz

1. See the official web site of Faiz Ahmed Faiz, http://faiz.com/.
2. See Kiernan, *Poems by Faiz*. For a more freewheeling translation of his poems, one could enjoy Agha Shahid Ali's *The Rebel's Silhouette* (Amherst: University of Massachusetts Press, 1995), and see one of its poems, 'The Dawn of Freedom', translated by Shahid in *Annual of Urdu Studies* 11 (1996), http://urdustudies.com/pdf/11/06dawn.pdf. I would also recommend Pritchett's essay on the craft of translation using Faiz as an example, 'The Sky, the Road, the Glass of Wine: On Translating Faiz,' *Annual of Urdu Studies* 15 (2000), http://www.urdustudies.com/pdf/15/07pritchett.pdf.
3. Ted Genoways discusses Faiz's prison poetry as reflected in his book *Dast-e Saba* in '"Let Them Snuff Out the Moon": Faiz Ahmed Faiz's Prison Lyrics in *Dast-e Saba*,' *Annual of Urdu Studies* 19 (2004), http://www.urdustudies.com/pdf/19/07GenowaysFaiz.pdf.
4. '*Aaj bazaar mein*' is available on YouTube, both in Faiz's own voice as well as sung by Nayyara Noor. '*Tum aaye ho na shab-e*

intezaar guzri hai' sung by Noorjehan is also available on YouTube. In Nandita Das's 2008 movie *Firaaq*, Naseeruddin Shah declaims '*Ye dagh dagh ujaala*'. Everyone loves Noorjehan's rendition of '*Mujh se pehli si mohabbat*', but let me also recommend the Fariha Parvez rendition, both of which are available on YouTube.

5. Faiz's metaphor reflects his incarceration, and he reads signs of his garden's (country's) fate from the breeze that eventually reaches his cage (prison cell).

Miraji

1. Geeta Patel's exhaustive book on Miraji combines context, biography and literary criticism: *Lyrical Movements, Historical Hauntings: On Gender, Colonialism, and Desire in Miraji's Urdu Poetry* (Stanford: Stanford University Press, 2002).

Ali Sardar Jafri

1. Sardar Jafri Foundation, 'Ali Sardar Jafri: Centenary Celebration of Ali Sardar Jafri,' http://www.sardarjafri.com/.
2. Syed Akbar Hyder, *Reliving Karbala: Martyrdom in South Asian Memory* (New York: Oxford University Press, 2006) 185–87.
3. This is an excerpt from the eponymous poem.

Jan Nisar Akhtar

1. Akhtar is also well known as the muse for some remarkably beautiful literary output; his wife Safiya's letters to him, well translated by Mehr Afshan Farooqi, are available at 'Letters to Jan Nisar Akhtar' by Safiya Akhtar, *Annual of Urdu Studies* 20 (2005), http://www.urdustudies.com/pdf/20/18SafiaAkhtar.pdf.
2. A recording of this can be accessed on YouTube.
3. This is an excerpt from a longer poem by the poet.

Majrooh Sultanpuri

1. One can view a recording of Majrooh's performance of this very ghazal at a mushaira on YouTube.
2. This is a classic progressive trope, condemning those who do not join the movement for social change. Kaifi had said: '*Jo door se toofan ka karte hain nazaara / Un ke liye toofan yahaan bhi hai, vahaan bhi*' ('Those who watch the storm from afar / For them, the storm is both here and there').

Kaifi Azmi

1. There is an official web page—http://www.kaifiyat.in—as well as a web page dedicated to him by the Library of Congress New Delhi Office at the South Asian Literary Recordings Project—http://www.loc.gov/acq/ovop/delhi/salrp/kaifiazmi.html. There are also assorted places like the website dedicated to the play *Kaifi aur Main*—http://www.kaifiaurmain.com/.
2. A translation of his poems into English by Pavan K. Varma was published in 2001 (Penguin).

Sahir Ludhianvi

1. In our book *Anthems of Resistance*, Ali Mir and I devote a chapter to Sahir which we have titled 'An Exemplary Progressive'. Also, see my article titled 'The Poetry of "No",' *Outlook* magazine (July 2004), http://www.outlookindia.com/article.aspx?224642.
2. Muhammad Sadiq, *A History of Urdu Literature*, 2nd ed. (New Delhi: Oxford University Press, 1984).

Sulaiman Khateeb

1. In 'Urdu's Progressive Wit: Sulaiman Khatib, Sarvar "Danda" and the Subaltern Satirists Who Spoke Up', Akbar Hyder suggests that not only were the Dakkani poets stigmatized by classicists in the field of Urdu poetry, but their progressive counterparts

also undermined their work, implicitly censoring all that was not written in a certain officialized Urdu. A new website dedicated to him—http://sulaimankhateeb.com/—contains a few audio and video files.

2. A *gampa* (untranslatable in English) is a multipurpose household appliance, a receptacle for carrying heavy stuff. Construction labourers carry sand and concrete on their heads in gampas.

Habib Jalib

1. See 'Ten Poems by Habib Jalib,' *Revolutionary Democracy* 9, no. 1 (April 2003), http://www.revolutionarydemocracy.org/rdv9n1/jalibpoems.htm.

2. Mansoor Hallaj was a Sufi mystic of Iran, who was famously executed in the tenth century by the Abbasid king Al-Muqtadir for putative heresy. Mansoor had proclaimed that God existed inside him, which was equated with polytheism. In Socratic fashion, Hallaj was executed for his steadfast refusal to recant his words. He is the patron saint of all martyr poets, after a fashion.

3. Here, Jalib shows how the progressive poets never abandoned the classical metaphors, especially Ghalib. These words come from a sher in a Ghalib ghazal, where he taunts those who do not understand him: '*Na sitaish ki tamanna, na sile ki parvaah / Gar nahin hai mere ash'aar mein maani, na sahi*' ('I desire neither praise nor recompense / And if my verses mean naught to you, so be it'). In the maqta as well, the term *shah ka masaahib* is derived from a Ghalib sher.

4. Implying they are written in the poet's blood.

Mustafa Zaidi

1. Laurel Steele's doctoral dissertation on Zaidi, titled 'Relocating the Postcolonial Self: Place, Metaphor, Memory and the Urdu Poetry of Mustafa Zaidi (1930–1970)' (University of Chicago, 2005) remains the definitive word on Zaidi in English. Her brief article on Zaidi, along with translations of six of his poems and

an elegy by Salam Machhlishahri can be found in the *Annual of Urdu Studies* 17 (2002), http://www.urdustudies.com/pdf/17/18_Steele.pdf.

Ahmed Faraz

1. Ali Mir's obituary of Faraz, 'Remembering Ahmad Faraz', containing a translation of a brief snippet from the poem, was published in the web section of *Outlook* magazine on 11 September 2008 at http://www.outlookindia.com/article.aspx?238364.
2. This can be heard in Faraz's own voice on YouTube.
3. Mehdi Hasan's rendition of this ghazal is considered to be the best. I would like to provoke the wrath of the purists and declare that I like Asha Bhonsle's version better. You can compare for yourselves as both renditions are available on YouTube.

Gulzar

1. This appears in the song *'Aane wala pal'* in the 1979 movie *Gol Maal*, and can be viewed on YouTube.
2. The song *'Is mod se jaate hain'* is from the 1975 film *Aandhi*. Gulzar's own rendition of the last poem was performed at the Vishwa Hindi Sammelan in New York in July 2007. Both are available on YouTube.

Shahryar

1. Qurratulain Hyder also won both awards, for fiction. A brief biography of Shahryar, followed by a translation of some of his poems by Rakhshanda Jalil, can be found in the *Annual of Urdu Studies* 17 (2002), http://www.urdustudies.com/pdf/17/19_Shahryar.pdf; while a recent obituary by Mehr Afshan Farooqi, 'Farewell, Shahryar', published in the web section of *Outlook* magazine on 21 February 2012, can be read here: http://www.outlookindia.com/article.aspx?279957.

Asif Raza

1. This sher is from Asif Raza's poem '*Amreeka*', and includes a reference to the legend of Prometheus, who was of course condemned for stealing the gods' fire.

Iftikhar Arif

1. Both poems have been performed by well-known artistes. The first qaseeda has been performed by Ali Haidar, and the second is a poem sung by Noorjehan; both performances can be viewed on YouTube.

S.M. Shahed

1. See: 'UrduShahkar,' http://urdushahkar.org/. The site also contains audio files of Shahed reciting his poems, including the one I have translated here. For his recitation of '*Fikr*', see 'Shahed: UrduShahkar,' http://urdushahkar.org/category/khudkalami/shahed/.

Javed Akhtar

1. Javed Akhtar, *Quiver*, translated by David Matthews (London: HarperCollins, 2001). Javed Akhtar's website, 'Javed Akhtar: Film Writer, Lyricist, Poet,' http://javedakhtar.com, is a great source of information and poetry about him. One must also recommend Nasreen Munni Kabeer's two books on him titled *Talking Films: Conversations on Hindi Cinema with Javed Akhtar* (New Delhi and New York: Oxford University Press, 1999), and especially *Talking Songs: Javed Akhtar in Conversation with Nasreen Munni Kabeer and Sixty Selected Songs* (New Delhi, Oxford, New York: Oxford University Press, 2005); the latter has many of Akhtar's film songs translated and transliterated.
2. See www.javedakhtar.com.

3. See 'Javed Akhtar's Quiver of Progressive Arrows: A Legacy Survives,' in *Anthems of Resistance*, 174–199, for an analysis of the non-film poetry, and chapters 6 and 7 for discussions of film lyrics.
4. The poet uses a pun, where *'usool'* can mean 'rule', but also connotes a sense of fairness and justice. The implied line is: 'if this is the rule, where is the justice?'
5. Another subtle pun—the term *'khel kya hai'*, in regular usage, implies 'what is really going on?'.

Fahmida Riaz

1. The English translations of her selected poems were published as *Four Walls and a Black Veil* (Karachi: Oxford University Press, 2004); other than poetry, her novella *Godavari* achieved great success, as did her volume of short stories, *Khat-e Marmuz*.
2. It appears in *Anthems of Resistance* [see 208–11. Also see 218–20 for long excerpts of her *'Kya Tum Poora Chaand Na Dekhoge?'* ('Will You Not See the Full Moon?')]. Her recent poem *'Bhagat Singh ki Moorat'* is available in Romanized script at 'Bhagat Singh ki Moorat by Fahmida Riaz,' Uddari Weblog, http://uddari. wordpress.com/2008/08/26/bhagat-singh-ki-moort-by-fahmida-riaz/, with an English translation by Riaz herself. Those wishing to see Riaz perform her own work can do so via YouTube.

Parveen Shakir

1. Five of her poems appear in competent English translation by Alamgir Hashmi at Cipher Journal, http://www.cipherjournal. com/html/hashmi.html. Do also read C.M. Naim's review article, 'Parveen Shakir: A Note and Twelve Poems,' *Annual of Urdu Studies* 8 (1993), http://www.urdustudies.com/pdf/ 08/20shakir.pdf.
2. There are several recordings of Parveen Shakir performing her own work, including the ghazal I have translated, that can be accessed on websites like YouTube.

Ishrat Afreen

1. See the official website of Ishrat Afreen, http://www.ishratafreen. com/.
2. One may read the translation of two of her poems along with a review essay by Nuzhat Abbas: 'Conversing to/with Shame: Translation and Gender in the Urdu Ghazal,' *Annual of Urdu Studies* 14 (1999), http://www.urdustudies.com/pdf/14/11abbasn.pdf.

Zeeshan Sahil

1. *An Evening of Caged Beasts: Seven Postmodernist Urdu Poets*, selected and introduced by Asif Farrukhi and translated by F.W. Pritchett and Asif Farrukhi (Karachi: Oxford University Press, 1999). A selection is available in the *Annual of Urdu Studies* 8 (1993), http://www.urdustudies.com/pdf/08/15evening_caged. pdf. Other than Sahil, the group comprised Afzal Ahmad Syed, Azra Abbas, Sarwat Hussain, Sara Shagufta, Tanveer Anjum and Saiduddin.
2. See: Zakintosh, 'Zeeshan Sahil: Lonely No More!' Windmills of My Mind, http://kidvai.blogspot.com/2008/04/evening-with-zeeshan-sahil-was-event.html. Also, five of Sahil's poems have been translated by Raza Ali Hasan and Christopher Kennedy for the *Annual of Urdu Studies* 21 (2006), and are available at http://www.urdustudies.com/pdf/21/16Zeeshan.pdf. I found a very brief audio clip of Sahil's voice at http://www.kidvai.com/windmills/Media/ZeeshansWish.mp3.

COPYRIGHT ACKNOWLEDGEMENTS

I would like to acknowledge gratefully the following for giving me permission to reproduce and translate some of the poems in this book. Gulzar, Javed Akhtar, Jameela Nishat, Ishrat Afreen, Fahmida Riaz, Iftikhar Arif, Asif Raza and S.M. Shahed permitted me to use their own work. In addition, I obtained permission from Fariha and Sambreen Rashed (for N.M. Rashid's poem); Saba Zaidi (for Mustafa Zaidi's poems); Tamkeen Khateeb (for Sulaiman Khateeb's poem); Shabana Azmi (for Kaifi Azmi's poems); Javed Akhtar (for Jan Nisar Akhtar's and Majaz's poems); Ali Nazim Jafri (for Ali Sardar Jafri's poems); Faridoon Shahryar (for Shahryar's poems); Ali Madeeh Hashmi and the Faiz Foundation (for Faiz's poems); Syed Abid Raza (for Zeeshan Sahil's poems); Parveen Qadir Agha, the Perveen Shakir Trust and Murad Publications (for Parveen Shakir's poem); Shibli and Saadi Faraz (for Ahmed Faraz's poems); and Andalib Sultanpuri (for Majrooh's poems).

While every possible effort has been made to contact the heirs of deceased poets, it has not been possible in all cases; I would be happy to include and acknowledge the heirs of any missed poets in future editions.